A HISTORY OF FELSTED SCHOOL; WITH SOME ACCOUNT OF THE FOUNDER AND HIS DESCENDANTS

A HISTORY OF FELSTED SCHOOL; WITH SOME ACCOUNT OF THE FOUNDER AND HIS DESCENDANTS

John Sargeaunt and Richard Rich (1st baron Rich.) and Rich family

www.General-Books.net

Publication Data:

Title: A History of Felsted School
Subtitle: With Some Account of the Founder and His Descendants
Author: John Sargeaunt and Richard Rich (1st Baron Rich.) and Rich Family
General Books publication date: 2009
Original publication date: 1889
Original Publisher: E. Durrant co.

How We Made This Book for You
We made this book exclusively for you using patented Print on Demand technology.
First we scanned the original rare book using a robot which automatically flipped and photographed each page.
We automated the typing, proof reading and design of this book using Optical Character Recognition (OCR) software on the scanned copy. That let us keep your cost as low as possible.
If a book is very old, worn and the type is faded, this can result in typos or missing text. This is also why our books don't have illustrations; the OCR software can't distinguish between an illustration and a smudge.
We understand how annoying typos, missing text or illustrations can be. That's why we provide a free digital copy of most books exactly as they were originally published. Simply go to our website (www.general-books.net) to check availability. And we provide a free trial membership in our book club so you can get free copies of other editions or related books.
OCR is not a perfect solution but we feel it's more important to make books available for a low price than not at all. So we warn readers on our website and in the descriptions we provide to book sellers that our books don't have illustrations and may have typos or missing text. We also provide excerpts from each book to book sellers and on our website so you can preview the quality of the book before buying it.
If you would prefer that we manually type, proof read and design your book so that it's perfect, we are happy to do that. Simply contact us for the cost.

1

A HISTORY OF FELSTED SCHOOL

PREFACE.

I HE writer of this small contribution to the History of Essex cannot hope to have escaped errors alike of omission and of commission. He must plead in excuse that the materials at his disposal have been both scanty and scattered, while his own leisure has not been large. He regrets that considerations of space have prevented him from adding exact references to the authorities which he has consulted. He must acknowledge many obligations for assistance in identifying persons. He has received special assistance from the Rev. F. H. Manlby, Rector of Broad

Somerford, who has made a careful study of the*J*

records of the School and the neighbourhood. Any

corrections and additions will be gratefully received.

SchoolHouse,

Felsted,

Sept., 1889.

Dublin, Trinity College. 32

Dunmow, Great, p. 113 sqq.

Dunmow, Little, p. 24, 118 sqq.

DyvesHall. 18

HISTOKY OF FELSTED SCHOOL.

ChapterI.

CHRONICLES OF THE SCHOOL.

T is perhaps hardly a cause for wonder that no History of Felsted School has yet been written. The materials for such a work are by no means large, and the result of much search must often be nothing more than a stray fact or a dubious inference. Yet the work is worth doing, and, imperfect as the present attempt must necessarily be, it may be hoped that from this beginning further search may supply the materials for a more adequate account.

Felsted School is directly an outcome of the Reformation. The earliest purpose of the founder is set forth in a deed dated April 26th, in the first and second year of Philip and Mary. In that year, 1554, the changes that followed the death of King Edward had made it possible for those who sympathised with. doctrines that he had discountenanced to express their piety in the forms that were pleasing to them. Prayers for the dead were no longer held illegal, and there was a revival of that spirit which had found its most

notable expression more than a century before in Archbishop Chichele's foundation of All Souls' College in Oxford. Sir Richard Rich, Knight, Lord Rich of Little Leez, had so far acceded to the measures of the Reformation as to act as Chancellor of the Court of Augmentations, and enrich himself with the spoil of abbey and priory. From 1547 to 1552 he had held the Great Seal, and had acquiesced in changes which he had perhaps regarded as for the time inevitable. With the reforms of doctrine and ritual which had commended themselves to Cranmer he had never agreed, and to this disagreement it was now possible for him to give an outward form. The monasteries had gone for good and all. There was no fear that Queen Mary would be able, however keenly she might desire, to restore to the black canons the gardens and fishponds and broad acres of the Priory of Leez. But the new owner might voluntarily restore a portion of his spoil to the purposes of the Church. If the monks had abused their trust and met with their deserts, there was no reason why a chaplaincy should not be endowed and masses be sung for the dead, as they had been sung in the Priory Church. Nor could Lord Rich forget that the alms of the monks, evil as these alms had been in their effects, must certainly be missed in the parishes which had enjoyed them. With such thoughts, he ordered the preparation of the first deed of the Felsted foundation. By this deed the chaplaincy was founded and provision made for the singing of masses and dirges and the ringing of bells in the Parish Church of Felsted. Thereto was added a Lenten dole of herrings to the parishioners of Felsted,

Little Leez, and Much Waltham. It might have been thought that Lord Rich's chaplain would have been posted at Little Leez. Doubtless the founder was induced to choose Felsted, not, as a modern might be, by its healthy and commanding situation, but by the size of its Church. He had already determined that in the aisle of Felsted Church should be the monumental chapel of his house, and the stipend of the chaplaincy might serve as an augmentation of the vicar's tithes. The endowment for these purposes was conveyed by a deed dated April 27th in the same year. It consisted of the rectories of Matching and Broomfield, with a farm at Morton, and the building which was afterwards known as the school house. The annual value of this endowment at the time seems to have been about thirty pounds. In this form the foundation continued throughout the reign of Mary.

The accession of Elizabeth led to the abolition of those observances which Lord Rich had enjoined. For some time the party opposed to reform cherished the hope that their views might even yet prevail; but, when it became clear that Elizabeth was firmly established on the throne, many of them began to reconsider their position. In 1564, Lord Rich was drawing towards the grave, and began to bethink him what he should establish in place of the abolished duties of the chaplain. That " convenable person," as he is described in the deeds, had still a function in connexion with the dole of herrings, but the rest of work had been " adnichillated " without hope of restoration. Though no reformer, Lord Rich was not unmoved by theexamples of Dean Colet and King Edward. Grammar schools were building in many parts of the land, for thus only could the wants of education be now supplied. Accordingly in May, 1564, Lord Rich ordered two deeds to be prepared for the establishment of a master and usher and the provision of their stipend. To the master was assigned an annuity of $20 out of Felsted Bury, while the usher was to receive yearly half as much out of the original endowment. A school was to be built on a narrow strip of land belonging to Lord Rich and lying between the churchyard and the public road. For this land a quit-rent was payable to the ground landlord, and such parts of the building as were not needed for the purposes of the school could be let as dwelling-houses and shops. It would seem that when these rooms should be wanted by the school the quit-rent was to cease, and the whole building become the absolute property of the foundation.

The place was well chosen for a school. High on the hill, which gave the village its name, it was perhaps the healthiest spot in the county. At once remote and accessible, it was even then not destitute of historic and architectural memories. From the Saxon tower of the Parish Church the scholar could look down on the aisle of the Priory Church of Little Dunmow, and the heaps of stones which marked the site of its conventual buildings. There too he might hope to see repeated the quaint custom of its ancient manor. On the other side the chimneys of Lord Rich's mansion rose amid the elms and willows of Sir Ralph Gernon's Priory at Leez. To the north were the spires of the nobleChurches of Thaxted and Stebbing. There too were the groves of Saling, where but a few years before Anne of Cleves, if tradition be true, had been well pleased to be forgotten. Far beyond was the stately castle of the De Veres, where half a century earlier the Earl of Oxford had learned to bis cost that loyalty would not atone for breaking the law. Eastward lay Braintree with its Keltic name, and through it passed the road by which Roman legions had marched to and fro between Camulodunum and Verulamium. Westward, if Camden's contention be right, was the site of their settlement at Csesaromagus, and the rampart of their entrenchment at

Canfield. Under the impulse of the new learning even a schoolboy may have paused to regard these traces of his predecessors.

In founding his school Lord Rich made provision, though in no very definite terms, for its government and administration. The chaplain and the churchwardens and parochians of Felsted were constituted into a corporation, but no powers were assigned to them in respect to the management of the school. Lord Rich had no thought of a time when his own line should come to an end and the palace which he had built pass into alien possession. The power of appointing and dismissing the chaplain and the usher, with the right to revise the accounts, was to remain with himself and his representatives after him. In modern phraseology, he and his representatives were to be the governing body of the school. In fact the rights of a governing body were exercised by Lord Rich in his lifetime and by his representatives after him till 1851. The form of education which was to be given in the school was also prescribed in the deeds. The subjects named are Latin, Greek, and Divinity. In other words, Lord Rich's intention was that his school should serve as a prelude to the University. It was thought that the school might accommodate eighty scholars, though the instruction of such a number, even in three subjects only, must have been no light task for two men. The school was to be called a free school, that is to say, admittance to its privileges was not to be limited by any such personal decisions as had been within the powers of the teaching monks. Whether any fees were paid by day boys must remain a doubtful question. In admittance to the school preference was to be given to boys born on Lord Rich's manors. These manors were very numerous and situated in all parts of the county. Provision was further made that on Whit-Sunday in every year a sermon should be preached in the parish church of Felsted by the vicar or his representative, who was to receive 13s. 4d. for his pains. At the end of the same year Lord Rich further established an almshouse for six persons and endowed it with the rectory lands of JBraintree and certain tithes from other lands of the foundation. The receipt of rents and tithes was assigned to the churchwardens of Felsted, who were to make their account yearly on Low Sunday to the representatives of the founder. Thus by the end of 1565 the foundation was established in the form in which it continued for more than two centuries and a half.

Unfortunately the chronicles of the first sixty years of the school's life are exceedingly scant. The very name of the first chaplain has been variously given. The historian of the County asserts that he was named Wharton, and possibly Mr. Wharton may have held the chaplaincy. Prom the records it may be judged that at any rate the first occupancy of the post must be ascribed to one Sir Henry Sayer or Sawer. It is however clear that Sir Henry, who, like Sir Hugh Evans and Sir Oliver Martext, owed his prefix to his holy orders, had ceased to be chaplain before the establishment of the school. He united with this office the chaplaincy of Lord Rich's chapel at E/ochford. The next name that appears in the records is that of Sir Thomas Rogerson. The school was founded in May, 1564. Some time in the following year the sum of $8 10s. was paid to Sir Thomas, but there is no reason to believe that he ever taught in the school. The first master of the school appears to have been named Dabney or Daubney. He held the mastership during the first quarter of 1566, but the real instauration of the school must be ascribed to his successor, John Berryman, of St. John's College, Cambridge.

Lord Rich died June 12th, 1567, and the accounts for the previous year were examined and signed by his son. As Berryman received only $14 for that year, there was probably a brief interregnum before his arrival at Felsted. It may be conjectured that his predecessor's appointment had been merely formal and temporary, and that after some enquiry Berryman, who had been twentieth out of forty-one honour men of his year,, was selected by Lord Rich.

We may form some idea of the character of the school in its early days. The head master resided in the house which had been assigned to him by the founder. This stood upon the same site as the house which was built at the beginning of this century, and used within the memory of many living Felstedians as the boarding house of the school. The older building was known as Ingrams, and there was payable for its use a yearly quitrent of threepence. This item appears in the accounts until 1632, when it seems to have been finally remitted. Of the number of boys who at first attended the school we have hardly any means of judging. The number of day boys can hardly have been large. The immediate neighbourhood may have been comparatively more populous than in modern times, but it is not likely that very many of the neighbouring farmers desired for their sons such an education as had been established by Lord Rich. He had, doubtless, had in mind how men like Chichele in one generation and Latimer in another had passed from the care of sheep to the cure of souls, and probably the ambition to do likewise was commoner then than now, but it must always have been rather the exception than the rule. Of boys who came from a distance it would be rash to conjecture that there was at first any great number. A boarding fee must of course have been charged, and this must have been a bar to many. Of the clergy, whose sons at a later time figured largely in the school lists, many were still celibate.' On the whole it is most unlikely that the school in those days reached the number named by the founder. Of those who came to the school, it is prohable that a considerable proportion passed as poor scholars to the Universities, especially to Cambridge. Many of these must have taken orders and afterwards held benefices both in Essex and elsewhere. Thus the danger, in which the cause of liberal education had been placed by the abolition of monastaries, was averted. To poor boys of ability there was given the same opportunity as before of rising from the lowest step to the highest, while there waa no pandering to meaner educational ends. Once only in the history of the school has there been a declension from its high ideal, and happily that declension was of brief endurance.

A few more facts connected with Berryman's mastership may be gathered from the records of the foundation. When he came he found the school buildings incomplete. To the usher had been assigned a chamber in the school and a garden, but as yet the chamber had no floor or ceiling and the garden was without a fence. In 1569, the patron ordered the necessary work to be done at a cost of $1 14s. 5d. The school was then in working order. The only place actually used for teaching was the large upper room in the school, where the chaplain sat at one end and the usher at the other. The rooms beneath were let, and unless Mr. Bycknor, the usher, remained all hours at his post, it may be presumed that Robert Evans and the three other tenants of the shop were at times conscious that the room above them was not unoccupied. Beside or beyond the usher's chamber there was another room or solar, and in 1571 Mr.

Berryman foundit advisable to hire this from the foundation. Since for this room there was exacted a rent, albeit but one shilling, it is probable that Mr. Berryman already had: among his boys some who were not of the foundation.

It is notable that even in these early days there was a trace of pluralism in connexion with the chaplaincy. For a brief space after 1568 Berryman held the living of Shelley on the gift of Lord Rich. In 1572 he resigned it for the living of Rochford in the same gift. He did not resign the mastership till 1576, and three years later he was inducted into the living of Dagenham. He died in 1617. His successor at Felsted was Henry Greenwood, a Yorkshireman by birth, and scholar and fellow of St. John's College, Cambridge. Further room was soon needed, and in 1580 the rooms and shops under the school were taken into the hands of the foundation. For what purpose they were used cannot be ascertained. It is most unlikely that they were employed as schoolrooms. The loss of rent involved was only 10s. 8d., and from this must be subtracted the half- crown that had been. yearly paid to the patron. Mr. Greenwood became vicar of Hatfield Peverel in 1596 and retired from, Felsted at Michaelmas in the following year. He afterwards held the livings of Little Leez and Great Sampford, and probably died before 1634. His successor at Felsted was Henry Manning, whose mastership is perhaps chiefly interesting from the fact that his son is the first Felsted boy whose handwriting has come down tous. On a fly leaf of the old account book of the foundation, where divers hands have scribbled scraps ofMartial and other writers, there appears, above the signature of F. Manning, a couplet which may possibly be his own: –

" Pergit in occasum quidquid provenit ab ortu:

Sera licet veniat mors ea recta venit." The date of these not very brilliant lines is 1606. The anti-papal spirit was already strong in the school. Among the fragments jotted down at this time are several epigrams on the Pope. Some of these were probably written by John Freeman, vicar of the parish, who may have encouraged young Manning in his poetical fancies. The last word of the following distich has been cut off: –

" Scilicet innocuus lupus ut grassatur in agris! Ut fremit! ut frendens faucibus ossa."

Further enquiry may shew whether these epigrams were original or transcribed.

At the time of Manning's death in 1627 the patronage of the school was in the hands of Robert Rich, second Earl of Warwick of this family. A zealous Presbyterian, and by birth, wealth, and character one of the leaders of the Puritan party, Lord Warwick was naturally anxious to find a master of character and ability who should be of like views with his own. The most distinguished Puritan teacher of that daywasJohn Preston, fellow, tutor, dean, and catechist of Queen's College, Cambridge. It would seem that to him Lord Warwick applied, and after an interval of some months the head mastership was assumed bj Martin Holbeach. The hour had come and the man.

Martin Holbeach was born in or near Banbury about the year 1600. He was a cadet of the house which has long flourished in that neighbourhood and is still seated at Farnborough, in Warwickshire. Preston was born at Heyford, in Northamptonshire, a village which is at no great distance from Farnborough, and it is probable that there was some connexion between the two Puritan families before the young Holbeach matriculated as a pupil of Preston in Queen's in the year 1617. He was followed hither in the next year by his younger brother Stephen, whose subsequent career has not been traced. The president of his college was one of the Davenants of Sible Hedingham, but Dr. Davenant was an ecclesiastical trimmer and in no way a man who can have had much influence over Holbeach. Preston, on the other hand, was a man all " judgment and gravity" and the most popular tutor of his time. He had sixteen fellow commoners, most of them heirs to fair estates, admitted to the college in one year. The Duke of Buckingham would fain have used him as a pivot to work the Puritan party withal, but Preston was at once too wary and too honest for the purpose. The pupil followed the master, and Holbeach was soon to be the most celebrated teacher of youthful Puritans. The circumstances of his appointment were in all ways favourable. The income of the foundation had just risen, and it was consequently possible to put the school buildings into thorough repair. In the political world the accession of Charles I. had given a more distinctly party character to the Puritans, while thewealth, as Clarendon says, and the views of Lord Warwick naturally pointed him out as their leader. Apparently there was at that time no other school in which they could place confidence, and they naturally turned to Felsted. Lord Rich had originally contemplated a school for eighty boys only, but as he had left the patronage and direction of the school in the hand of his successors, this ordinance could be varied. It cannot be proved that any other than Essex boys were received into the school before Holbeach's time, but there can be no doubt that Lord Rich's great grandson gave Holbeach leave to receive boys from all parts of the country. Of the state of the school, four years after his appointment, we have the testimony of one of his most distinguished pupils. " At Christmas, 1630," says Wallis, " I was sent to school to Mr. Martin Holbitch, at Felsted, in Essex, who was a very good schoolmaster. At this school, though in a country village, he had at that time an hundred or six score scholars, most of them strangers sent thither from other places upon the reputation of the school, from which many good scholars were sent to the University." How entirely the reputation of the school was due to Mr. Holbeach is shown by the fact that Lord Rich was already forgotten, and Wallis deemed the school to be of the foundation of the Earl of Warwick. Wallis himself was of the strangers, for he was born in Kent. It is probable that before he-left he made the acquaintance among the small boys of Robert Cromwell. Unfortunately it is impossible to recover the names of most of the six score scholarsand upward who were his contemporaries. Stray notices in divers places give us a few names. Here were many of the Mildmays, a distinguished Essex family, distantly akin to the Puritan founder of Emmanuel College. Here was William Viscount Fairfax, of Elmley, a Yorkshire Puritan, though his mother was a Howard. Here too were Robert Cromwell's hrothers. Men of this stamp were little liked hy stout Royalists. Sir John Bramston, who had a special quarrel with Henry Mildmay, and who seldom let his veracity obstruct his spite, wrote years afterwards of his opponent that " he was bred under Holbech, scholemaster at Felsted, whoe scarce bred any man that was loyall to his prince." To Bramston, it seemed that Mildmay had " suckt in from his master's tuition principles of disloyaltie and rebellion." That Sir John's view was jaundiced is proved by Holbeach's treatment of Isaac Barrow Isaac, though an uncompromising Royalist, found special favour in his master's eyes.

We may suppose that during the two and twenty years of Holbeach's mastership there were not a few distinguished visitors to Felsted. It is known that Oliver Cromwell occasionally found time to visit his wife's relations and thence divert to see his boys at school. Before the end of Holbeach's term not a few of the more distinguished puritan clergy were men who had been boys under him. Of those who had been at other schools, many must have looked for counsel to the man who was in sage counsel old. Leagued with him was a friend of his college days, Edmund Calamy, one of the authors of Smectymnuus and now reader at Rochford. Calamy was a frequent visitor at Leez, in whose owner he found, in his own words, "-a pattern ior all."

Meantime at Felsted the promise of riches had not been maintained. The expenses had risen more than in proportion to the rise of income, and the necessary repairs of school and school house had been done partly at Holbeach's own cost. Of this he could scarce complain, for the deficit had been in some sort caused by a rise in his own stipend. From the time of his appointment he had been assigned by Lord Warwick's order a yearly income of thirty pounds. However, in 1638 the lease of Broomfield fell in. Holbeach not only received back his disbursements but also had his salary raised to fifty pounds. The usher's income at the same time was raised to twenty-five pounds. At these figures the stipends remained for half a century.

We have shown Holbeach as a vigorous and popular schoolmaster. Unfortunately there is another side to the picture. We have lightly set aside the sneer of Sir John Bramston, but there is other evidence of Holbeach's character which cannot be so easily gainsaid. Arthur Wilson, the historian, was perhaps the most fair-minded man of his time, and there is extant a letter of his addressed to Holbeach, in which more in sorrow than in anger he beseeches the schoolmaster to mend his ways. Acknowledging his belief in Holbeach's sincerity, he points out that his zeal were none the worse for a leaven of Christian charity. The. strifes and discussions of " our poore village " and outbreaks of fanaticism, wherein vehemence was not tempered by love, were unhesitatingly ascribed to Holbeach's influence, and an appeal was made to him to heal the wounds which he had caused. The effect of this letter we do not know, but it is clear that there was a very nnamiable side to Holbeach's character.

His subordinates had been of like temper with himself. Mr. Seton, the first usher of his appointment, went away to preach throughout the county, and found little favour in the eyes of his ecclesiastical superiors. In 1630 was framed a list of " such ministers in Essex as are not conformable in opinion nor practice." Fifth, among eleven names, comes " Mr. Seton, now or late usher to the schole in Felsted, in the deanry of Dunmow; a bold boy and unlicensed." Laud did not yet foresee that Holbeach's bold boys would be more than a match for him in the end.

In 1649 Holbeach's long and prosperous mastership came to an end. Appointed to the vicarage of High Easter, he at once took a leading part among the beneficed clergy of the county, acting as an ordaining presbyter and as one of the commissioners for the removal of scandalous and inefficient ministers. In an official return of the period he is described as " a very godly and learned divine," a character which stood him in little stead at the Restoration. Ejected from his benefice under the Act of Uniformity, he retired to Dunmow, and, dying in 1670, was buried at Felsted. His tombstone, standing in Lydiatt's time, cannot now be found. He had married a wife, and twelve years later Mrs. Lydia Holbeach was laid by his side.

Prom the entrance registers of the Cambridge Colleges, which contain many names of Holbeach's pupils, it is possible to form some view of the state of the school at this time. It contained boys of many different grades. The sons of peers and country squires sat cheek by jowl with the sons of farmers and tradesmen. Of intermediate social rank were the sons of the clergy, who formed the larger part of the school. Probably many sons of squires did not go to the Universities, while those who did frequently took no degree. Boys of scantier means went as sizars to Cambridge, took a degree, and in many cases were ordained. If he failed to obtain a fellowship, such a boy returned to fill a small incumbency in his own county. Of course there was no such thing as would now-a-days be called a modern education; the clergyman and the tradesman had to choose for their sons between a classical education and no education at all. The principle had its disadvantages, but the Cambridge system of sizarships at least placed a liberal education within the reach of all but the poorest of the peasantry. The state of education may be not inaptly compared with the system of schools and universities in Scotland at the present day.

It is probable that Mr. Holbeach had a voice in the appointment of his successor, and it is also probable that this successor was one of his own pupils. As usual, there was a brief interregnum, the reins being in the hands of one Skingle, but at Lady Day, 1650, Mr. Christopher Glascock took up his residence in the School House. He was a member of an ancient Essex

family, long seated at Dyves' Hall, and was himself lord of the manor of Bedel's Hall, in Writtle, and master of a school at Ipswich. He was about three and thirty at the date of his appointment, and may, perhaps, have been Holbeach's favourite among his earliest pupils. He went to St. Catherine's Hall, Cambridge, and took his degree of B. A. there in 1634. As Holbeach took his furniture with him to High Easter, though if he dwelt in the vicarage of those days he must have been satisfied with scant space, his successor received from the foundation ten pounds towards the cost of his removing. He was destined to preside for forty years over the fortunes of the school and to maintain its traditions. Among his pupils were the sons of the chief families in the county, and the sons of distinguished puritans from other parts. Among them were some or all of the sons of Gilbert Holies, Earl of Clare, the unrelenting opponent of the Stuarts. His second son William, who fell at the age of twenty, at the siege of Luxemburgh, gave to the school a volume which is still in its possession. Mr. Glascock maintained his faith through the evil days of the Restoration, and though he lived long enough to see the patronage of the school pass into alien hands he may have found some consolation in seeing James II. driven from the country which he had outraged. Mr. Glascock survived the Restoration little more than a twelvemonth, and Lord Nottingham, in that terrible January of 1690, when, Tory though he was, he was using all his energies to dissuade William from abdicating the throne, received the news that it had

become his duty to appoint a master to Pelsted School. Lord Nottingham's wife had been Lady Essex Rich, daughter of the third Earl of Warwick, and for reasons which cannot now be ascertained, her sisters, Lady Anne Barrington and Lady Mary

St. John, had surrendered to her their share in the patronage. In one way this was fortunate, for Lord Nottingham was a man of the highest character. Honesty was rare among public men, but the bitterest Whig would not now impeach Lord Nottingham's. On the other hand, lie had, of course, little sympathy with the traditions of the school, and we may presume that the man of his choice was of Tory and High Church views. Simon Lydiatt, a Christ Church man of some thirty summers, came after three months' interval, and soon showed that, whatever his political and ecclesiastical theories may have been, he was, at any rate, not lacking in scholarship or activity. He was zealously supported by his patron through a somewhat trying time. The difficulties that he had to meet were legal and financial. The lease of Broomfield parsonage fell in, and Sir John Pock, the tenant, requested a renewal thereof at the old rent. He based his request on a clause in the lease, and represented that the low rent was really a compensation for tenant's improvements. Lydiatt thought that ample compensation had already been made; land was more valuable and the rent must rise. Sir John vowed he would pay the old rent or none, and in fact paid none. The chaplain appealed to the patron, the patron took the whole burden on his own shoulders, and both sides went to law. On Nottingham's generositythe chaplain might have quoted some lines written by a pupil of his predecessor and acquaintance of his own:

" Manet cui cura paterna Proteget has pecudes, ipsos pecudumque magistros."

The foundation sued for a writ of ejectment against Sir John, and Sir John would fain have compelled a renewal of the lease. Meantime no rent was paid, and the stipends of chaplain and usher suffered accordingly. After eighteen months the case came to trial and the Lord Keeper decided against Sir John. The pertinacious tenant appealed and had his deserts, for the former decree was confirmed and Sir John cast in arrears and costs. Sir John, having much faith in the law's delay, again refused payment. Another suit followed, and then at the end of six years my Lord Keeper showed his teeth and Sir John reluctantly succumbed. Of the three hundred and fifty pounds paid as arrears of rent half went to Lydiatt and ninetyfour pounds ten shillings to the poor usher.

Such faith had Lydiatt in the success of his suit that he had already sought leave from Lord Nottingham to build a gallery in the west end of the parish church. Part of the twenty pounds which it cost was raised by felling timber. The gallery remained till the restoration of the church by the present Vicar in 1876, though it had long ere that proved too small for its purpose. Better memorials of the chaplain's taste were coats of arms, which seem now to have disappeared. His zeal was not without guerdon, for from the increased rents his salary was raised by ten pounds.

Another memorial of Lydiatt's time is the only complete school list of the last century that has come down to us. It exists in manuscript in the University Library at Cambridge. It is the list for Christmas, 1710, and we believe it to be in the handwriting of Mr. Woodroffe, the vicar of the parish. Although some of the names are mere shadows, enough may be identified to tell us something of the sources from which the boys were drawn. It contains sixty-four names, and most of the boys were the sons of Essex squires and clergymen. A few came from Suffolk, while it is probable that some of those who have not been identified were strangers in the land. Perhaps most were sons of Tory parents, but the Aylmers must have been Whigs. They were not all happy, for two. we learn, in that December, " ran from school." It should seem that they did not run far.

From a manuscript diary of affairs in those Christmas holidays we gain some insight into the life of the village. The diary is probably the vicar's, a gentleman given, like Laud, to recording his dreams. " On Saturday night, as near as I can remember, I had the dream about the King." As Queen Anne was still alive we may ask, what King? " Friday morning, about 6 of the clock, dreamt about gold and plu: at Mr. St: For: Hall." The gentleman is doubtless Mr. Stane, of Forest Hall, but whether plu: be plush is a question to be asked. We learn how Mr. Price, the usher, was given to coursing, and how at Mr. Lydiatt's one evening there was dancing and music. Clearly there were changes since Holbeach ruled at Felsted. Moreover, there were dinner parties and some intercourse with Lord Manchester's family at Leez and talk of other things than had busied men's minds three score years before.

Some time before Lydiatt had found time to edit a collection of Greek epigrams which he called Stachyologia or Spicilegium. The book was well got up and reached its fourth edition in 1738. He was afraid that it might be reproached as a very little work, and threw the blame on the publishers, who were unwilling " libri magis gravidi periculum facere." The work is described as " in usum scholae Felstediensis com. Essexiae," and dedicated to Lord Nottingham, " patrono munifico." Lord Nottingham had indeed done more than his duty to the school, though it does not appear that he sent to it any of his thirty-one children.

The school feast was also an institution of Lydiatt's, and he preached the first sermon thereat. It was. dropped by his successor, but afterwards intermittently revived. Once, in 1795, it is recorded that the feast was put off on account of " the then scarcity and high price of provisions." It may be hoped that the present O. F. dinner in London will be of more regular occurrence.

A dark cloud obscured the close of Lydiatt's prosperous reign. The terrible disease, from whose dread no man in those days was free, and which but a few years before had thrown most of the nation into mourning for a beloved Queen, fell upon Felsted. In October, 1711, the smallpox broke out in the school. We know how badly the disease was treated in thosedays and may imagine Lydiatt's helpless efforts to mitigate the force of the blow. He did his best to keep the school together, but it was not till the following April that the plague was stayed. Meantime the school had suffered much " prejudice and loss," and Lydiatt's health had broken down under the strain. In the following November he died. He had served the foundation well, and was spared the knowledge that his successor was to be less able than himself.

Hugh Hutchin, who was appointed to the chaplaincy at Christmas, 1712, was, like his predecessor, an Oxford man. As an undergraduate he was at Lincoln College, from which he graduated in 1698. By some means he attracted the attention of Aldrich, who induced him to remove to Christ Church, where he held a chaplaincy. He was also pro-proctor, and sometime before 1706 was appointed Master of the Cathedral School at Christ Church. Meantime he had published an edition of Justin Martyr's Apology, and done some other literary work. He is described as a good-natured man, of quick parts and proportionable learning. It was probably on Aldrich's recommendation that Lord Nottingham appointed him to Felsted. He may have been glad to leave Oxford, where he had not escaped the small squabbles and jealousies which then did little honour to the University. From the fact that he had projected but never completed an edition of Polybius, he got the nickname of Pol Hutchin, which probably did not follow him to Felsted. The history of his mastership is very obscure. The testimony of Cook's life proves him a good teacher, but he was perhaps not a man to make himself popular. He dropped the school feast, and it is probable that the numbers of the school went down. Nothing more can now be ascertained. Mr. Hntchin died in March, 1725, and was succeeded by Mr. John Wyatt. Over the coming period there is much temptation to draw the veil. It was an epoch of pluralism and degradation, of idleness and neglect. The consequence was inevitable, and the time of recovery long and tedious. Wyatt was the son of William Wyatt, Principal of St. Mary's Hall, Oxford, and was about six and twenty at the time of his appointment. At first he did not neglect the school, and it is to his credit that among his earlier pupils was Thomas Townson. His income was, perhaps, not very large, and the temptation to accept livings may have been considerable, but he must have known that in holding his mastership with them he was violating the terms of his appointment. Unfortunately Lord Nottingham died in 1731, and his successors had little care for the interests of the school. The head master was probably the same John Wyatt who in that year was inducted into the vicarage of Hatfield Peverel. Certainly he was afterwards rector of Little Waltham, and became in 1747 perpetual curate of Little Dunmow. The school sank in numbers, and when in 1750 Wyatt died there were only nine boys in all. In the face of these facts we may fairly distrust the eulogy of his epitaph in Little Waltham church. He is there said to have been "revered and loved by his scholars, and esteemed by all that knew him for his learning, integrity, piety, and charity." It was, perhaps, this inscription that led his successor to describe him as " a man of great abilities, learning, and integrity." But Dr. Drake also was no enemy to pluralism. The ushers of this period were no less-eager for incumbencies. Hans de Veil was vicar of Saling from 1732 and of Felsted from 1740 till his death in the following year. Mark Gretton had the vicarages of Good Easter and Margaret Roding for fifteen years before his death. During six of those years he was also usher of the school. However, the ushers' income was very small, and for them there might be some excuse. It could scarce require two masters to teach nine boys.

Mr. Drake was twenty-seven when he came to Felsted. He was a son of the celebrated Francis Drake, author of Bboracum, who lived many years after his son's appointment to Felsted. The son was born at York, and was probably a boy at St Peter's School. In 1741 he matriculated at Christ Church, proceeded B. A. in 1744, and took orders. He became usher of the third form at Westminster, and came to Felsted 10th April, 1750. His salary was but sixtyfour pounds, and the profits of nine boys. The total income of the trust was $170, and for a time Drake can hardly have seemed on the high road to wealth. However, he was an active man, and made a vigorous effort to revive the school. In 1753 the school feast was revived with Sir John Tyrrell and Stephen-Skynner as stewards and John "Woodrooffe preacher. As a very large number of gentlemen are said to have attended, it may be presumed that the school was recovering its fame. Drake had already brought to the Bchool, as usher, William Drake of King's. The usher's parentage has not been traced, but he was probably a cousin of the chaplain. After another year the feast dropped, to be revived again in 1763 and 1764. Perhaps the best of Drake's pupils at this time was Samuel Massingberd, who went to Oxford and obtained a fellowship at Magdalen. At Christmas, 1774, he returned to the school as usher. He did not remain long, but went to America, where he was. drowned, about two years later, in the river Delaware.

In 1766 Drake was appointed to the vicarage of Layer Marney, but in those days of pluralities he did not resign the mastership of the school. Indeed he found time to contribute papers to Archeeologia, being now also a fellow of the Society of Antiquaries. Hereby he made himself some name, and had his reward in 1777, when he was appointed to the vicarage of Isleworth, and at Lady-Day following, resigned his mastership to William Trivett. He lived at Isleworth till 1801, and the Annual Register in its obituary notice describes him as "a gentleman well known in the literary world as a scholar and antiquary."

In Drake's time we trace the beginning of a connexion between the school and Wales. John Meyricke, of St. Mar in Pembrokeshire, was a Felsted boy in 1753. There were several Welsh boys under Trivett, of whom the most notable was Lord Dinorben, and the connexion, for which in those days it is difficult to account, has continued intermittently to the present time.

With the accession of the Rev. William Trivett a new era of prosperity dawned upon the school. He was born in 1745, at Leicester, where his father was in no very exalted station of life. At the age of eighteen the young Trivett was sent to Christ Church, where he seems to have won some reputation. From Oxford he went to Westminster as usher of the fourth form. During the ten years that he spent at that school he seems to have formed a wide connexion among the parents of the boys who passed under his hands. When he came to Felsted in 1778, he attracted boys from all parts of the county. The school was soon as widely known as in the days of Holbeach, and Wynns and Hughes' from Wales sat in class beside Freres from Norfolk, and Bramstons of Essex. Some of these boys remained for the whole of their school time at Felsted; to others the school served as a parvise to the larger edifice of Eton. Hughes and Jackson completed their school days at Felsted, the Freres went to Eton. Trivett seems to have been exceedingly popular with his pupils, and it may have been at the suggestion of some of them that in 1792 he revived the school feast. Five years before he had been instituted to the vicarages of Arlingdon and Willingdon in Sussex, and as his years were now approaching' fifty, more than half of which he had spent in teaching, he began to turn his eyes towards repose. In his view this repose was not to be obtained in Sussex. He therefore left his curate in charge and devoted himself with considerable success to the accumulation of incumbencies. He had probably married before he left Westminster, and having now ason old enough to be ordained, saw little limit to the possibilities of clerical endowment. In 1810 he was inducted to the rectories of Penshurst and Ashburnham in Kent. The scenery of that county pleased his fastidious taste, and he seems thenceforth to have resided at one of his incumbencies. There he remained fat and well liking, and attained to four score years and five. Of his doings in 1811 we have some account in the-diary of Sir George Jackson, a younger brother of Francis James Jackson. " Francis and a body of old Felstedians – Bramston, Hughes, Kynaston, Bartle Frere, and others – have been getting their former head master, old

Trivett, up to town and giving him a round of dinners. Wednesday will be our turn. I say *your*, because, though not of Felsted, I shall dine with the Felsted party. The old boy looks remarkably well, Francis says as well as when he first saw him thirty years ago. He is about to get possession of a third living adjoining the two he now holds, in addition to Maldon, so I think he is pretty well off. His son stays in the country to take care of the duty. He, too, has done pretty well, for in one month he had the offer of a living in Sussex of $330 per annum, of two in Suffolk, one about $500 with residence, and another of $150 without. From the favour of old pupils and of patrons they are always, it seems, in a similar puzzle. It is with them a continual embarras de richesses. It is no bad thing to be a popular head master."

The " old boy" had, no doubt, a reason to be pleased with himself, though his idea of clerical duty would hardly satisfy a more critical age. He could at leastpoint to the success of his teaching as shown in the success of his pupils. In a small school he had trained at least two brilliant scholars, two distinguished statesmen, two or three eminent diplomatists, and other men of some mark. Perhaps he did well to be satisfied. He died in 1830.

With Trivett's retirement the line of Christ Church masters came to an end. His successor, William John Carless, was of Merton College, and had been for a little while head master of Chigwell Grammar School. The time was not altogether favourable. The war had begun to tell on the resources of the country, and in 1795 it was found necessary to put off the school feast on account of the then scarcity and high price of provisions. The wide connexion which Trivett had formed seems to have ceased with his departure, and his successor was thrown back upon the resources of the county. The old building known as Ingrams had fallen grievously out of repair, and improved means of communication were not altogether in the school's favour. However, Carless was young and hopeful, and he determined to make a gallant effort to maintain the high name of the school. At the school feast on August 25th, 1796, it was proposed and unanimously agreed to " (1) That it is essential to the prosperity of this ancient foundation that the master's house be completely repaired and rebuilt. (2) That the members for the county, together with any gentlemen who have been educated at the school, be desired to wait upon the patron, the Earl of Winchilsea, and request his lordship's sentiments upon the best mode of effecting thisobject." His lordship, who was a bachelor, was a grandson of the great Earl of Nottingham, who had served the school so well a century before, and his sentiments took the form of a cheque for $650. To this he afterwards added the sum of $77 14s. Further, he allowed the rent of the farm at Morton to be set aside for the rebuilding. To this was added by subscriptions, chiefly of old boys, $757 11s. The list was headed by Colonel Bullock, M. P. for the county, who, like six other Old Festedians, gave five and twenty guineas. The other member for the county, Mr. Eliab Hervey, was not a Felstedian, and declined to subscribe. A committee was formed, with T. B. Bramston at its head, and the work was put in hand. The first brick of the new house was laid April 1st, 1799, by Mr. Carless. The work took about two years. In addition to the original plan the head master spent a considerable sum on the house and the brewhouse adjoining it. Despite his liberality it was found at the end of 1801 that there was a considerable deficit, and Mr. Bramston made a further appeal for subscriptions. Nearly $200 more was raised, and the committee presented their final report in April, 1803. In the two following years a further sum of $122 18s. 6l d. was raised to put the playing field in order.

Mr. Carless further revived and extended the school library. It had been established in 1601 by the purchase of seven books. The gifts of old Felstedians had added many folios to its shelves, but it was defective in modern and general literature. A subscription library was started, and many of the books then purchased are now in the school library, In the changes and neglect of later years they were sadly wounded and battered, and it must be confessed that, though they are now treated with affectionate care, they were not always so selected as to tempt either the learned or the lazy reader. The subscriptions seem to have ceased with the death of Mr. Carless, but the library has since been revived and now threatens to overflow the space allotted to it.

It might have been thought that after so much energy and liberality the school would rise in numbers. Such does not seem to have been the case, except perhaps for a brief period. The chronicles at this epoch are almost a blank, but when Mr. Carless died in 1813 there were only twenty-two boys in the school. Such at least was the number found by his successor. Yet Mr. Carless had done a good work, and though the names of most of his boys are lost, it is known that he had under him at least one eminent scholar.

For a hundred and twenty-three years the school had been under Oxford men. Mr. Edmund Squire, who assumed the chaplaincy in 1813, was of Christ's College, Cambridge, where he had graduated twelve years before. The records of the school throw little light on the two and twenty years of his mastership. Something may, however, be gathered from other sources. He was at first eminently successful, but an unfortunate quarrel with a family of great influence in the county made him generally unpopular, and the fortunes of the school came to a low ebb. Mr. Justice Denman, who is one of the few living pupils of Mr. Squire, has borne genial testimony to his teaching, and to the mathematic zeal of Mr. James Crocker, his usher. In the early years of his mastership he published a small book on Greek verses, which reached a second edition before his death.

On the death of Lord Winchilsea in 1826, the patronage of the school passed to his cousin, Mr. Finch, of Burley-on-the-Hill. There was no eager competition in 1835 for the vacant chaplaincy, and it was at length filled by the appointment of Dr. Surridge, of Trinity College, Dublin. The nomination was eccentric, but, though the immediate results were disastrous, it happened that Dr. Surridge was able to confer a great boon on the foundation. The Doctor, who was on the high road to fifty, had been a navy chaplain, and, if he had ever possessed any scholarship, had forgotten it in climbing up the climbing wave. It is related of him that at the school feast of 1836 he boldly converted an alcaic line into the semblance of a fragmentary hexameter, and the ears of Felsted scholars were startled by "vimprom&vet insitam." Had he been conscious of his crime, the Doctor need hardly have wondered that the sons of the squires and clergy sought their culture elsewhere than at Felsted. Perhaps it was the want of pupils that induced him to search the records of the foundation. Whatever may have been the motive of his search, he learned in it that a considerable portion of the income of the foundation had been misappropriated. This had been done purely by inadvertence, and when the patron's attention was called to the fact he at once took steps to remedythe wrong which he had unwittingly done. Application was made to the Attorney-General, and as the result of a snit in chancery, the income of the foundation was very largely raised. With the means thus placed at his disposal, Dr. Sarridge once more made an effort to revive the school. Perceiving that he was not able to maintain the traditions of the school, he made up his mind to alter the form of education which was prescribed by the school deeds. The system of free scholars had never been very successful, and for a long time had been practically extinct. This system he attempted to revive, but a country village is not the place for such a school as he desired, and the number of scholars whom he attracted was very small. It is perhaps unnecessary to say that though Dr. Surridge professed to be carrying out the wishes of the founder, he was in fact doing the very opposite. He was severing all connexion between the school and the Universities, and diverting the income of the trust to an alien purpose. Meantime he had developed a pugnacious spirit which brought him much trouble. A bitter quarrel with Mr. Kirby, the usher, ended in the chaplain's appealing to the patron, by whom the usher was dismissed in 1843. A squabble with the churchwardens on the question of building an organ in the gallery of the church brought about the interference of the higher ecclesiastical powers. With creditable impartiality, Dr. Snrridge wrote in the school records that both the churchwardens and himself were rebuked. It was clearly advisable that he should make way for a more competent man. The income of the foundation

was now large enough to make provision for his old age, and in July, 1850, he retired upon an annual pension of $200. The last entry in the churchwarden's account book records the appointment of his successor. Mr. A. H. Wratislaw, the last headmaster appointed by the representatives of the founder, was a fellow and tutor of Christ's. He had been third classic and a senior optime in 1844. He started with two and twenty boys, and the school may be said to have been revived under his mastership. The discoveries of Dr. Surridge had called attention to the inadequate superintendence of the school, and steps had already been taken to procure an Act of Parliament on the subject. The object of the act was to establish a governing body, and to renew that connexion of the school, as a place of liberal culture, with the Universities, which had subsisted for nearly three centuries, but had been driven into abeyance by the vagaries of Dr. Surridge. The events of subsequent years are of too recent occurrence to be more than briefly sketched in this place. As to the character of this governing body, opinions differ. While some of its members were hardly such as could deal effectively with educational interests, and dim stories linger of tradesmen who, in its early times, found the profit of their place, it cannot be denied that they did much to meet the growing requirements of the school. In 1855, Mr. Wratislaw migrated to Bury St. Edmund's, and subsequently became vicar of Manorbier, Pembrokeshire. Under his successor, Mr. W. S. Grignon, of Trinity College, Cambridge, who had been fifth classic in 1846, the

school outgrew the old buildings and the old playground. It was determined to build anew, and by degrees the new school rose on the new site, while the old school house was ultimately sold. In the church, the gallery was no longer able to hold all its rightful occupants, who overflowed even the large chancel and its precincts. In 1867 an appeal was made for a subscription to build a chapel. At the end of five years a considerable sum had been raised, and by the addition of certain fees and school funds the amount was raised to $3,000. The chapel was opened on Founder's day, 1873. In the same year an organ was built, at. a cost of $244. In 1875, the pulpit, the altar rails, and the lectern were added, and the mosaic floor within the altar rails was given by J. J. Tnfnell, Esq. Painted windows have since been put into the chancel in memory of W. E. P. Hamilton, V. C., of Francis Grepp, and of the Queen's Jubilee. The fresco at the west end is a memorial to R. R. Winter, and the chancel walls were painted in 1886. Mr. Grignon ceased to be head master in 1875, and, after a brief interval, was succeeded by Mr. D. S. Ingram, of St. John's College, Cambridge, thirteenth classic in 1862, and lately second master of Blundell's School, Tiverton. Tinder Mr. Ingram considerable additions have been made to the school buildings. The cricket pavilion was built in 1879 and the gymnasium in 1883, while the cricket ground has been enlarged by the incorporation of the field which had been occupied for more than three centuries by the almshouse kine. Mention must also be made of two benefactions of recent years. In

36 HISTORY OF FELSTED SCHOOL

1869 T. W. Bramston, Esq., whose constituents had subscribed a large sum to present him with his portrait and a testimonial on his retiring from the representation of South Essex, patriotically chose to benefit his old school rather than himself. The sum of $600 was invested in the funds, and a prize founded, which is known by his name. In 1882 another prize was founded in honour of Mr. Grignon.

Lastly, it should be added that in 1876 the scheme of the Court of Chancery was repealed by the Charity Commissioners, and that the school is now under a governing body which is representative of the whole county.

elucidation of documents written in cipher. Such writing was even commoner in those days than in our own, largely as it is still employed in despatches and telegrams. However, few people were acquainted with more than one system, the commonest being that employed thirty years later by Pepys, and Wallis made it his business to understand all systems. From Felsted in 1632 he went to Emmanuel College, Cambridge. At Felsted he had been fretting that he was not earlier sent to that University, but he now acknowledged his mistake, for so much better was the teaching of Felsted than the system pursued at Cambridge, that he was able to keep pace with those who were considerably older than himself. He was soon chosen scholar of Emmanuel, but as by the statutes he could not at that time be elected to a fellowship, he migrated to Queen's. At Queen's he held a fellowship till, in 1644, he married Susanna Glyde, of Northiam.

In politics Wallis was a decided Royalist, and had the courage to protest against the execution of King Charles and " the errors, heresies, and blasphemies of the times." It would seem, however, that despite this protest he did not irrevocably commit himself against the government. At any rate he was no high churchman, for the bigoted but worthy Hearne in after years complained that he had always been an admirer of fanatics and Presbyterians. It would seem a confirmation of this, and of Hearne's further statement that he was a man of revolution principles, that he lent his skill to the deciphering of the king's cabinet. After, or possibly before this " worthy work," as the goodantiquary ironically styles it, he was appointed by the Parliamentary

Commissioners to succeed the ejected Dr. Turner in the Savilian professorship of geometry at Oxford. During the Commonwealth he pursued his studies in geometry and divinity, engaging, among other controversies, in one with Hobbes on the squaring of the circle. He was also skilled in the civil law, and his enemies said that he had such a trick of sophistical evasion that he would make black white and white black. The said enemies naturally thought that this was his recommendation to Cromwell, who, at any rate, had much respect for him, and got him appointed custodian of the University archives. An impartial observer might have supposed that his skill in deciphering had something to do with the appointment.

About this time his active mind was directed to experiments undertaken with a view to make the deaf and dumb to speak. He tried his plan on one Whalley, of Northampton, who had been deaf and dumb from his birth, and in a few months he displayed Whalley loquacious to one of those gatherings of savants from which sprang the Royal Society. The remainder of his career was a long one, and apparently no less active than that of his earlier years. His last work was some emendations, allowed by unfriendly Hearne to be very good, to Avienus' account of the world. Some time before his death, his picture, drawn to the life, was put in the schools' gallery, and the old man went to see it in its place, an act which Hearne stigmatises as due to vanity. The evident animus of the antiquary makes his acknowledgment of Wallis's parts all the morestriking. He was " deservedly accounted the greatest person in the profession of mathematics of any of his time. He was withall a good divine, and no mean critik in the Greek and Latin tongues." Hearne also tells us that Wallis " when he was fourscore years of age, or near it, could purely by the help of his memory multiply 20 numbers by 20, and then extract the cube root." Hearne might well call this " an instance of his extraordinary parts."

Dr. Wallis died at Oxford, in 1703, at the age of 87. His only son married an Oxfordshire heiress. Of his two daughters, the younger married William Benson, of Towcester, and died without offspring in 1700, while the elder became the wife of Mr. Serjeant (afterwards Sir John) Blencowe, of Marston St. Lawrence. The present squire of Marston is directly descended from Dr. Wallis, a distinction which he shares with many of the Northamptonshire gentry.'

II. – THE CROMWELLS.

Very close was the relation of the great Protector to Felsted School. Himself, of course, a native of Huntingdonshire, his wife, Elizabeth, whom he married in 1620, was the daughter of Sir James Bourchier, who would seem to have been a London merchant. Sir James owned by inheritance, or more probably by purchase, the ancient manor of Grandcourts, situate in Felsted parish, between Felsted and Bayne. It is not improbable that Oliver Cromwell, in the course of his connexion with Cambridge and his acquaintance with John Preston, was soon after his marriage brought intocontact with Martin Holbeach. At any rate in his visits to this neighbourhood and his intimacy with Lord Warwick he mnst have known something of Felsted before his boys were of an age to be sent to school. Moreover, his own manifold concerns had induced him to allow the boys to spend a considerable part of their earliest youth under the roof of their grandparents at Grandcourts. It cannot be said for certain whether the boys resided with Sir James or were boarders in the school house, the ancient edifice known to the olden records as "Ingrams," on the site of which now stands the house occupied by Mr. Williams. As the house of Grandcourts, is some three miles from the school it is probable that the boys lived in the school house and spent their " exeats," if the Puritan would admit such vanities, under their grandfather's roof. At Felsted, Robert Cromwell died at the age of eighteen. A death among the boys of Felsted has happily been an occurrence of extraordinary rarity. The only other recorded instance is that of the young Sir Charles Tyrrell near the beginning of the last century. It would seem that Bobert Cromwell was one of those whom heaven loves, for he has note in the parish register as " eximie pius juvenis, deum timens supra multos." His next brother, Oliver, was more than a year younger and apparently was also at Felsted at the time, and, living long enough to serve as a cornet of horse in the civil war, came to a mysterious end in 1644. It is now generally held that the evidence proves the young soldier to have died of the small-pox.

Whether a good or an evil thing for the country, it was certainly an unhappy thing for Richard Cromwell that the death of his elder brothers made him his father's heir. He only of Cromwell's sons would seem to have inherited no spark of his father's genius, and but a faint glimmering of the family strenuousness of spirit. A feeble soldier and an idle lawyer, he had more regard to the sports of the field, and even therein there is no record that he excelled, save the record of an enemy to sport. Perhaps it was his knowledge of the young man's weakness that made Cromwell at first most unwilling to have his office established hereditary in his house. The ambiguity of his nomination and the story of the sealed document at the critical time not forthcoming are well known. It boots not to follow his further career or relate how the foolish Ishbosheth was impotent to grasp his father's sceptre, or how when the mouse ran up the clock, the clock struck one, the mouse ran down, dickory, dickory, dock! At the age of 55 he came back from his exile to live, pseudonymous and retired, till he died at Cheshunt in 1712. Bighty-and-six was he when he died, and had seen four kings and two queens upon the English throne.

Of other and better stuff was Henry, the Protector's fourth son and fifth child. He served with distinction in the latter years of the civil war, and not wholly to his father's delight was appointed, in 1654, MajorGeneral of the forces in Ireland. The truculent policy of his race was but little modified in the administration of Henry Cromwell. Some toleration there was for Roman Catholics, but deportation and exportation, ruthless, measureless. In June, 1659, he was recalled by the Parliament, and on the restoration was allowed to retire to his own part of the country and live in retirement at Spinney Abbey, in Cambridgeshire. He died in 1674, leaving a large family, of whom sprang numerous descendants.

In reference to the local associations of the Cromwells, it is worth noting that no connexion can be traced between the family of Sir James Bourchier and the house called Bourchiers close to Felsted station. Bourchiers is in the possession of Mr. Hastings Worrin, and from the deeds connected with the property it is clear that at no time was it in the possession of the iamily whose name it bears.

III. – ISAAC BARROW.

Of all the worthies who have gone out from Felsted none can take a higher place than Isaac Barrow. Scholar and mathematician, controversialist and man of science, preacher and theologian, he touched nothing that he did not adorn. Sprung of a Suffolk family that had migrated to Cambridgeshire, born in 1630, he was sent at an early age to the Charterhouse. Here he would none of books, and not only spent his own time in fighting but was the cause that fighting was in others. Indeed his "reports" were so bad that his father, linendraper to King Charles and perhaps, poor man, getting but little pay in those stormy times, was heard to say that if a son of his must die he could best spare Isaac. Hereupon some wise friend suggested thathis school should be changed. There was the school at Felsted, which Mr. Martin Holbeach was fast raising to fame. True, Mr. Holbeach was of Puritan views, but the Long Parliament had not yet met and there was no war to the knife. So good Mr. Holbeach had a new pupil and found him apt. Judicious handling turned' the pugnacious lad into a notable schoolboy, and Mr. Holbeach gave him charge of the studies of a little schoolfellow of Yorkshire birth, Lord Fairfax, of Elmley. Mr. Holbeach was too wise to try and break his boys into his own views, and doubtless there was nmcli wordy war between the young Royalist and his Puritan associates, Bourchiers and Cromwells, and perhaps younger scions of the house of Rich. In 1643 Barrow was entered at Peterhouse, where his uncle was Fellow, but before he could go up the two-handed engine had smitten, and his uncle had been ejected. Hence when Isaac went to Cambridge, he found himself under Puritan rule and a pensioner at Trinity. His father had followed the fortunes or misfortunes of the King, and the boy must have left Cambridge but for the contributions of Royalist divines. Dr. Hammond and his friends must have been astonished to find a young ally coming from the great nest of the enemy at Felsted. Yet he did not lose the respect of his adversaries, and the Master of his College dubbed him a good lad, and patting him on the head added that it was a pity he was a Royalist. Clearly it was noordinary lad that could then win the favour of both parties and remain steadfast to the cause of his love.

Elected in 1647 Scholar, and in 1649 Fellow, of THnity, Ray, of Black Notley, being chosen with him, he was thought of in 1654 for the vacant professorship of Greek. Rejected for a Puritan and older candidate and weary of Cambridge Puritanism, the young fellow set out on his travels. At Paris he found his father well nigh penniless, and did somewhat to help the decayed man of linen. To Italy, to Smyrna, to Constantinople, falling in with pirates and remembering to good purpose his fights at Charterhouse and Pelsted, went Isaac, and after biding a year's space among the Ottomans, he returned to find old Noll dead and men's eyes turning to Breda. When the King had his own again, Barrow had the professorship coveted but missed aforetime. He became, moreover, a cleric and professor of geometry at Gresham College, but soon discovered that he " could not make a Bible out of his Euclid" and so resigned to Newton. In 16,72, he succeeded Pearson as Master of Trinity, and lived such for a lustre. Then in lodgings in London, after preaching for some hours, as was his wont, in Guildhall Chapel, he fell sick, and dying, was buried in Westminster Abbey.

It is said of him that he was of uncouth bearing, lean, pale, and short. He smoked much and ate ravenously of fruit. He rose early and walked before breakfast. Probably he had been given to birds' nesting at Pelsted. One morning in the garden of a house where he was staying he met a mastiff, and the mastiff his match, for the lean divine pinned the dogand might have slain him, had he willed. Reflecting that the beast had done but his duty, he held him unharmed till others came. Could we desire a better testimonial to the strength of his body and the gentleness of his son!?

Barrow's great mathematical works were written in Latin, a custom now, alas, honoured in the breach. His last biographer says that he had almost a mania for turning everything into Latin verse. Let us hope that so harmless a form of insanity is still to be found within Felsted walls.

IV. – THOMAS COX.

It cannot be absolutely proved that Thomas Cox was a Felsted boy. He was the preacher at the third Felsted feast, which was in 1709, and as there were many old boys who had taken orders it is most unlikely that a stranger should have been chosen to preach. Moreover he held the living of Broomfield, of which the rectory belonged to the foundation. The time and place of his birth have not been ascertained. From 1680 to 1704 he held the living of Chignal Smealy. Thereto he added 1685 the vicarage of Broomfield, and in 1703 the rectory of Stock Harvard. In the Felsted records he is mentioned merely as vicar of Broomfield, where in all probability he lived. He was a man of considerable culture and a voluminous pen. His most important work was a lengthy supplement to Camden's Britannia. This was published in numbers during thelatter years of his life. His Felsted sermon was also published. Its text was not ill chosen: " Moses was learned in all the wisdom of the Egyptians, and was mighty in words and in deeds."

Cox married Love Man wood, the daughter of one of his parishioners at Broomfield, and died in 1734, leaving one son. He must have been over four score ere he died.

V. – SIR JOHN COMYNS.

The exact date of the birth of John Comyns has not been recorded. He is said to have been born at Dagenham, in this county, about the year 1665. His father was a barrister, and his mother of the house of the Rudds of Little Baddow. His father's family was not without influence in the county, though none of them seem to have risen to special eminence. Comyns came to Felsted under the prolonged headmastership of Mr. Christopher Glascock, when the school, without entirely losing its old Puritan character, had become the place of education of all the chief families in the county. No account of his school life has been preserved. At the age of about eighteen he seems to have gone to Queen's College, Cambridge, and soon afterwards to London to read for the bar, to which he was called in 1690. He soon won himself reputation, rather for legal learning than for any special brilliancy. In 1701 he was elected Member of Parliament forMaldon, and continued so with a brief interval till 1713. Mean

time, in 1704, he received the Serjeant's coif. At the second of the Felsted School feasts, held in 1708, he, with Charles Tyrrell, Esq., a member of a very ancient Essex family, held the post of steward. After a brief return to political life, he was appointed in 1726 one of the Barons of the Exchequer. In 1736 he was transferred to the Common Pleas, but two years later he returned to the former court as Chief Baron. He died in 1740, and his body lies in Writtle Church. To the last he kept up his connexion with Felsted, and about the year 1735 presented to the school library a copy of Stephanas' Thesaurus.

Comyns was devoted to his profession, and his career was devoid of notable incident. He was thrice married, but as he left no children his estate of Highlands, near

Chelmsford, passed to his nephew. The legal works which he published have always maintained the highest authority. According to Lord Kenyon, he was accounted by his contemporaries the ablest lawyer in Westminster Hall. His books were written in that law French to whose ill-sounding jargon Milton in his Tractate of Education compared the smattering of Latin with an English tongue. They have been translated and many times republished, and in their new dress have more than gained in usefulness what they lost in quaintness.

Though no leader of men, Comyns found a place to fill, and filled it with distinction to himself and benefit to his country. Therein, in no small measure, lies the strength of nations.

VI. – THOMAS COOKE.

Born in 1703, the son of a Mnggletonian innkeeper at Braintree, Thomas Cooke was sent to Felsted probably about the time when Mr. Hugh Hutchin succeeded Mr. Lydiatt as head master. By some means he obtained the notice of Lord Pembroke, who saw that the boy had taste and encouraged him in his rapid progress in the classics. In the preface to his translation of Hesiod, a copy of the second edition of which work, presented by himself, is now in the school library, he natters the Lord of Wilton with all the fnlsomeness of his time. In 1722 the young scholar went to London and attached himself to the literary society of the disciples of Addison. After writing a poem on the death of Marlborough and a translation of Moschus and Bion, he naturally fell foul of the Tory coterie that gathered round Pope at Twickenham. Proving successfully the not very difficult thesis that the little Papist had less Greek than might have been looked for in a translator of Homer, he prepared for himself a place in the Dunciad. The goddess of Dulness decked her imps as men of fame and

" Cook shall be Prior and Concanen Swift." Hereupon Cooke reissued his former volume with notes more and more biting than before. He had not always this courage, or, as is not impossible, Pope lied. Pope asserts that Cooke libelled him hi sundry journals and wrote privately to deny the authorship of the libels. But as usual the poet bas two accounts of the same event.

" Pitholeon sends to me: ' You know his Grace,
I want a patron, ask him for a place.'
Pitholeon libelled me – ' but here's a letter
Informs you, sir, 'twas when he knew no better.' "

The earlier commentators and Cooke's last biographer assume that our worthy is the man referred to in another part of Pope's Prologue to the Satires: –

" From these the world will judge of men and books, Not from the Burnets, Oldwixons, and Cooks."

The late Rector of Lincoln has, however, adduced good reason for supposing that not Thomas Cooke but Roger Coke is here alluded to. It is, however, not impossible that Cooke's " Scandalous Chronicle" may give him a claim to be the object of Pope's Satire.

Cooke still pursued with much vigour his literary career, and in 1728 he published that translation of Hesiod which gave him the nickname of Hesiod Cooke. The work was dedicated to John, Duke of Argyle and Greenwich, the patriotic peer of Scott's Heart of Midlothian, and to George, Marquis of Annandale. Cooke also projected a translation of Plautus, and, according to Dr. Johnson, lived for twenty years on it, always taking subscriptions but never publishing. The Doctor, on the same occasion, told Boswell how Cooke once presented Foote to a club in the following singular manner: – " This is the nephew of the gentleman who was lately hung in chains for murdering his brother." In 1754 Cooke did actually publish a translation of one play of Plautus, the Amphitryon. Before this he had written sundry plays, all of which would seem to have been with more or less emphasis damned. In politics he appears to have joined the dissentient Whigs who followed Pulteney; and when Amhurst died neglected and broken-hearted, Cooke sncceeded him in the editorship of the " Craftsman." He had chosen the losing side. The skilful management of Pelham destroyed all but the semblance of an opposition, and Cooke, robbed of all support, fell into great poverty, wherein in 1756 he died in a small house in Lambeth. He left his manuscripts to Sir Joseph Mawbey, the foolish Member of Parliament, " at whose speeches and whose pigstyes the wits of Brooke's were in the habit of laughing most unmercifully," and Sir Joseph long years afterwards contributed many anecdotes of his friend to the " Gentleman's Magazine." Cooke left one daughter, of whose career prorsus tacendum est.

VII. – DR. THOMAS TOWNSON.

Dr. Townson was a man whom his contemporaries delighted to honour, but it may be feared that his glory in these later days has somewhat paled. His name and works are still known to the learned, and deserve to be more widely celebrated. With the help of his friend and biographer, Ralph Churton, of Brasenose, we may set forth some of his claims to remembrance. He was born in 1715, the eldest son of John Townson, rector of Great Leighs, and Lucretia his wife. After the wont ofthe time he was placed under the care of a neighbouring clergyman, Henry Nott, of Terling, whence he was sent to Felsted, then under the headmastership of Mr. Wyatt (1725-1750). In 1733 he was entered a commoner at Christ Church. In July, 1735, he was elected Demy, and two years later Fellow, of Magdalen; was ordained deacon in 1741, and priest in 1742 by Seeker. Three days later he started for the continent, apparently as " bear-leader " to one Mr. Dawkins. He spent about eight months in France, a year and a half in Italy, and eight months more in Germany and Holland, landing at Harwich just a week after Charles Edward had raised the banner of insurrection in Glen Finnan. On his return he became tutor of his college and vicar of Hatfield Peverel, a living which in 1749 he resigned for that of Blithfield in Staffordshire; but he would seem to have resided at neither place. However, in 1751, he quitted Oxford to become incumbent of the lower mediety of Malpas in Cheshire. In 1758 he inherited a legacy of eight thousand pounds from an old friend of his father's, William Barcroft, rector of Fairsted, and vicar of Kelvedon. He was an exemplary parish priest, and devoted his leisure to the writing of books. His sermons, says Churton, were of "mild persuasive eloquence," and his delivery had " the meekness of majesty." Once his ministry was interrupted. In 1768 he went abroad with the son of his patron, William Drake of Ma'pas. When after a year's absence he came back to his parish, his parishioners flocked to meet him, and every one that saw him blessed him. His character no less than hislearning must have deserved the honorary degree of D. D., which in 1779 his University conferred upon him. Two years later, Bishop Porteus, of Chester, induced him to accept the

Archdeaconry of Richmond. The old man may well have hesitated in accepting the post, for his next year's commission compelled him to ride nearly six hundred miles. In 1783, Lord North offered him the Regius Professorship of Divinity, but this he declined. But though he could not undertake such work, his old age was green and vigorous. When he had passed his seventy-fifth birthday, he sent a Latin poem to his friend, the younger Drake. It was the time of the French Revolution, and the old man mourned the change in the land which he and his friend had together visited: –

" Gens levis, gens sunt malefida Galli,
Sed fides antiqua beatiorem
Anglica terra relinet tuoque
Pectore sedem."

The expression is not quite perfect, but the friendship is evidently real. In the autumn of 1791 his health failed, and, for the first time since he came to Malpas, he called in a doctor. This desperate remedy was not immediately fatal; but in April 15th, 1792, he passed peacefully away. Townson's Discourses on the Gospels were honoured with the special commendation of Routh; and worse sermons have been preached even in these later days.

VIII. – WILLIAM BARKER DANIEL.

If Felsted can claim in Dr. Townson one of the most learned of English divines, we mnst not from any fear of the contrast omit the name of one of the most eccentric of clerics. Whence Daniel came we do not know, but as a precocious schoolboy of ten summers or thereabouts he recited an English copy of verses at the Felsted speech day in 1763. He left school some time later and went no man knows whither. He was nearly thirty when he appeared at Cambridge, where he graduated in 1787. It is probable that he had been on sporting bent, and when he took orders he did not lay aside his gun. He held no benefice, and the only recorded occasion whereon he preached is the Felsted feast day in 1792. Nine years later he published the work on which his reputation rests. He called it " Rural Sports," and it ran through several editions in a short time. Old sportsmen are still to be found in whose eyes there are but two books, the Bible and Rural Sports. However, the profits of the work were not large enough to recoup the cost whereby the writer had gained his experience. Daniel found it necessary to confine himself to the limits of the King's Bench. Stung with the charge that he was but a Nimrod in prunella, or hopeful of more gains from a fresh venture, he published from his prison some thoughts on the Lord's Prayer. His training had not fitted him for religious literature, and none but a biographer could now read his discourses. He died in 1833, being as was supposed four score years of age.

IX. AND X. – THE LORDS DINORBEN AND WESTERN.

These two worthies may, from the likeness of their careers, fitly be classed together. They were born in the same year, they were at school together, they were many years in Parliament, they were of like political views, they were both raised to the peerage and neither founded an abiding house.

WilliamLewisHugheswas born in 1767, the eldest son of the Rev. Edward Hughes, of Kenmell Park, Denbighshire, whose wife was the heiress of Llystulas, Anglesey. He entered the school under the mastership of Mr. Trivett, and apparently completed his education at Felsted. In 1802 he was elected member for Wallingford, in the first Parliament of the United Kingdom. As a zealous Whig he kept his seat for nine and twenty years, and through the dark times when the country was groaning " Beneath the sway Of Sidmouth and of Castlereagh," of Perceval and Liverpool, he fought bravely under the banner of a suffering minority. With his son-inlaw, Lord Gardner, he was a member of the coterie that gathered round the Duke of Sussex, with whom he was associated in Freemasonry and other high aims. In 1811 he was one of a company of old Felstedians who invited Mr. Trivett to London and entertained him with a round of dinners. In 1816 he was steward of the Felsted feast. In such work he was in his element. The present writerhas it on the authority of an ancient relative, who was a friend of the worthy Felstedian, that in later days he was so fond of good living that his intimates, punning on his title, dubbed him. Lord Dinner-bell. When the Whigs came back to power, the member for Wallingford reaped the reward of his constancy, if reward it was. On the coronation of William IV. in 1831 he was raised to the peerage as Baron Dinorben, of Kenmell Park. He had married in 1804 a daughter of Ralph W. Gray, by whom he had nine daughters and one son. His wife died in 1835, and his son a few years later. He married again in his old age, and his daughter by the second marriage became the wife of- Sir Arundell Neave, of Dagnam Park. Lord Dinorben died in 1852, and his only surviving son in the same year.

CharlesCallisWesternwas born in 1767, the eldest son of Charles Western, Esq., of Rivenhall, near Witham. He was for a little while at Felsted, but like William Frere and others of his contemporaries, spent the later days of his school life at Eton. He is reputed to have been at Cambridge, but seems to have taken no degree. In 1790 he was elected M. P. forMaldon, and with a brief interval in 1806 and 1807 remained such till 1812. In 1801 he was a large subscriber to the Felsted building fund. In 1812 he contested the county of Essex as a Whig, and being elected after a hard contest retained his seat for twenty years. He was also chairman of Quarter Session and a zealous agriculturist. Although a Whig he was, like many others of his party, a firmbeliever in protection. He helped to frame and vigorously supported the wretched corn law of 1815, the proximate cause of the misery of thirty years. He was, however, firm in the cause of Parliamentary Reform, and in presenting the Essex county petition in favour of the Reform Bill came into conflict with his Tory colleague, Mr. Tyrrell. The zeal of Essex for Reform did not extend to gratitude, and in 1833 Mr. Western lost his seat for the county. Lord John Russell immediately induced Lord Grey to offer him a peerage, and he took the title of Baron Western of * Rivenhall. His last years were spent in opposing free trade, and he died in 1844, on the eve of its triumph. Lord Western was never married.

XI. – FRANCISJAMESJACKSON.

Jacksonwas born in 1770, a son of Thomas Jackson, rector of Yarlington and canon of Westminster. He came to Felsted about 1781 and remained there till 1786. He was then taken from school to enter active life in the diplomatic service. In 1791 he was appointed Minister Plenipotentiary at the court of Spain. Thence in the following year he sent to the school library a magnificently bound copy of the Infante Don Gabriell's sumptuously printed translation of Sallust. Young though he was, his skill in diplomacy had already won for him the firm support of more than one minister, and the success of his career seemed assured. In 1801 Addington sent him to act as minister at Paris, while Cornwallis was negociating the terms of peace atAmiens. Re-called from France in April, 1802, he was sent in the following September to be minister at Berlin. Here he remained for three years and a half, and was supposed to enjoy, ia a very high degree, the confidence of the varions powers. Here, too, he found a wife, Elizabeth Dorville, danghter of the lord steward of the court of the late Elizabeth of Prussia. When in 1807 it was feared that Napoleon would appropriate the Danish fleet, Jackson was sent to induce the Danish Government to surrender their ships under a pledge of restitution. It was hardly likely that even the persona grata of the old Felstedian would succeed in so unprecedented a demand. Count Bernstoff and the Prince Royal received him, the one with vehement indignation, the other with stately courage. Jackson harried back to England to be the first to bring the news that the English fleet was bombarding Copenhagen. It was impossible for him not lo sympathise with the national feelings of the Danes, but apart from his duty as a diplomatist he must have seen that the danger of England left him no choice but to carry out his instructions.

In August, 1809, when troubles arose with America and the English Government declined to ratify the convention of Erskine, our envoy in that country, Jackson was chosen to succeed him. It was thought that he was the man most likely to avert an unnatural war. After a tedious voyage of fifty-three days he lauded in America to find prejudice so strong that his task was hopeless. He remained firm in the face of indignation and insult, and withdrew with dignity froma position where success was impossible. Soon after his return his health began to give way. He lived chiefly at Brighton, Buffering much from the physicians, but cheerful under his pain. He wrote to his brother that there was nothing left of him but a shadow, but he would think of the song " Luff, boys, luff," and hope for better days. The hope was vain, and he died still a young man in August, 1814.

Jackson's letters to his mother bewray an official mind but on the whole an affectionate nature. He sometimes took his mother to task for babbling of state secrets, and once was much troubled that a letter of his was delivered to the wrong Mrs. Jackson and read forthwith. Happily the letter had not fallen into evil hands and his official reputation escaped unscathed.

XII. – EGBERT FBL LOWES.

RobertFelloweswas born at Danbury in 1771. His father was of the family that is seated at Shottesham Hall, in Norfolk. With his elder brother William he was sent to Felsted about 1780. Eight years later he went to Oriel, but did not take a degree till 1796, when he had become a member of St. Mary's Hall. He afterwards took orders and became editor of the "Critical Review." Liberal clergymen were rare in those days, and Fellowes' political views, which were like those of his friend Dr. Parr, met with little favour in the eyes of his clerical brethren. He was not, however, deterred from supporting such projects as the London University, and the legacy of a large fortune

60 HISTORY OF FELSTED SCHOOL

from a friend enabled him to support them with effect. In his later days his theological views underwent a change which would have made it difficult for him to hold a benefice. He had no desire to perform clerical work and was still bent on philanthropical schemes, when he was seized by his last illness. He died in 1847, leaving a family. Of his numerous works very few are now found in the hands of readers.

XIII. – BARTHOLOMEW FRERE.

There were at Felsted at least three members of the family of Frere, which is seated at Roydon Hall, near Diss. Bartholomew was the younger brother of John Hookham and William, and was born in 1776. At school he seems to have made the acquaintance of Francis Jackson, who was more than five years his senior. Going to Trinity College, Cambridge, he there greatly distinguished himself. In 1798 he won two Browne's medals for a Greek ode and for epigrams. In the following year he was Chancellor's Medallist, and took his degree as head of the Senior Optimes. In 1801 he was appointed secretary to the legation at Lisbon, whence he was transferred in 1809 to Spain. Here he was smitten by the charms of an Andalusian damsel and aspired vainly to her hand. His friends thought that he was neglecting politics for love, and urged him to depart from the Peninsula. In 1811 he went toTurkey as secretary of the embassy. He had 40 years more of life, but remained faithful to his first love, and died a bachelor in 1851.

ChapterIII.

THERECORDSOPTHEFOUNDATION.

F the original deeds of the Foundation something has been said in the former chapter. In addition to these ancient parchments there are in the custody of the Head Master two volumes of great and varied interest. One of them contains the churchwardens' accounts of the moneys and corn received and disbursed from 1566 to 1710, with occasional notes of other occurrences. The second book is a continuation of the first down to 1842, and contains various and desultory records of events in the history of the school. On the cover of the former volume is a note in the handwriting of Dr. Surridge. " This book, which had been deposited for safety in the Foundation Chest, was unaccountably abstracted therefrom, and did not appear before the Commissioners of Charities, but was,*subsequently to their inquiry,*handed from a shelf in the almshouses to the late chaplain, Mr. Squire, who in 1835 handed it to his successor, Dr. Surridge." Part of the material of these volumes is used in other parts of this work. In the present chapter some account isgiven of matters of more general interest, both. historical and philological. To show the form of the volume the first year's accounts are printed entire, except the entries mentioned within brackets: –

The accompt of Thomas Nevell and Thomas Bredge, churchwardens of the paryshe church of felsted and receyvers of the rents of the lands and tents of the foundacion of the Bight honourable Richard Riche, knight, Lord Riche, for the sustentacion of the poore within the paryshe of felsted, made and yelded up uppon Lowe sundey in the nynthe yere of the reigne of our sovereygne Ladie quene Elizabeth as foloweth First receyved of Robert Eton fermor of the parsonage of Bromefielde for one hoole yees rent ended at the feast of Seynt michaell tharchangell last past xviiilbvi' xa

It rec of William Glaskocke gent
fermor of the parsonage of matching for one hoole yeres rent ended
at the seid feast ixlbiv" vid

It rec of Thomas Gryggs for one
hoole yeres rent of Steyn lands
ended at the seid feast iiilbvi* viii4
It remeyning in our hands from the
last accompt as appereth by the
same xviis
Summa totius receptionis xxxiiiilbv*
These be the charges of the seid wardens touching the seid foundacion as followeth
First paid for XI barels of heryng xivlbvi8vidIt pd for XI cads of Shoten red
heryngs It pd for the cariage of the saime
from maiden to felsted It pd to the churchwardens of muche
waltham for there peynes It pd to the churchwardens of litle
lees
It pd for a pay boke
It pd to Robert Albert for XI dales
work of hym and his man for
tyling the skole howse It pd for one thosand of tyle for the
same howse
It pd for carrying two loads of sand
It pd for a packe of tyle pynnes
It pd for one thosand of lath neyle
It pd for a quarter of lyme
It pd to the ussher of the skole for
his stipent for iii quarters ended at
the feast of the natyof our lord
god last past It pd to the churchwardens of felsted
for their paynes
It pd for our dynner at thaccompt
rCawfell for makyng a
sermon Whit sundey
It to the clerke
It to the sexton
It pd to the vicar of Bromefelde for
one hoole yeres pension
It pd for procurations of Bromefeld
parsonage xvi" viid
It paid mrstrangman for rent of the
foundation house iii
It pd for makyng the boke xii4
It pd to the vicar of felsted vi8viii4
Summa totius solucionis
So remayneth The accompt of the seid wardens touching the yearly annuytie to
them graunted out of felsted bury. First receyved of the Bight honorable
the seid Lord Riche by the hands
of Humfrey Rowland gent receyver

to the seid Lord Riche for one hoole
yeres annuytie ended at the feast
of Seynt Michell tharchangell last
past xx1"
Whereof pd to mrDabney skolemr
for one quarters wages ended at
the feast of thannunciation of
our Ladie anno dmi 1566 v"1
It paid to mrBeryman for one other
quarter ended at the feast of the
natyof Seynt Ihn bap* iiii1*
It pd to hym for one other quarter
ended at michas last past vlb
It pd to hym for one other quarter
ended at the feast of the natyof
our Lord god last past vlb
Summa totius solicionis xixlb
So remayneth xx1
The accompt of the seid wardens touching the almes house as foloweth –
First recey ved of Christoph er Gooddey
for one hoole yores rent of the
parsonage of Branktre ended at
the feast of Seynt Michaell tharch
angell last past xxmxxd
Whereof pd to the almes folkes the
viithdaie of Aprill ao dmi 1566 for
every of them one monthes wages xxii*
It pd to them allso the vithdaie of
May for every of them one other
monthes wages xxii'
[The same sum was paid on June 2nd and 30th, July 22nd, August 25th, September
22nd, October 20th, November 17th, and December 15th.]
It pd to them allso the xiithdaie of
January for one other monthe xviii" viii*
It pd to them allso the ixthof
February for one other monthe xxii'
[The same was paid on March 9th and April 6th.]
It pd for a latteys for the corne solles
wyndow vii*
It for our peynes v"
Summa totius solucionis xvlbx" iii*
So there remeyneth iiiilbxi" vd
The accompt of the seid wardens tuching the wheat and malt to them appoynted
First receyved of Robert Eton from the vithdaie of octobre ao dm 1565 untill the
xii1'1daie of decembre1566 of wheat iii quarters iiii busshels of malt v

quarters iiii busshels. It rec of mrGlaskocke for the same tyme of wheat
iii quarters iiii busshels It of malt vi quarters one busshel It rec of John Gooddey
for the same time of wheate
iii quarters of malt iii quarters Summa of all the wheate receyved during the seid
tyme is x quarters and of malt xiiii quarters 5.
busshels
Whereof delyvered to the Almes folk of the same. as foloweth First delyvered to
them the vii daie of Aprile for
one monthe of wheate iiii busshels of malt vi
busshels
[The same amount was delivered on May 6th, June 2nd and 30th, July 22nd, Aug.
25th, Sept. 22nd, Oct. 20th, Nov. 17th, Dec. 15, Jan. 12th, Feb. 9th, March 9th,
April 6th.]
Summa of all the wheate delyvered to the Almes folk is vii quarters and of malt x
quarters and a half
(And they did sell besyde this allowance xviii busshels of malt so remeyneth of
wheate iii quarters and of malt xv busshels.
Item the foreseid churchewardens have delyvered to the Almose folks of the said
foundacion by the commandement of the right honorable the lorde Riche within the
time of this accompt to be soldo and employed for and towarde the relief of the same
Almose folk in malt xviii bushels
Summa totalis of all the cxpence and delyvries of the said wheate and malt within
the tyme
aforesaid
wheat vii quarters
malt xii quarters vi busshels
Remayning in thands of the said churchewardens the vitbdaye of Aprill an" ix-
moregine Elizabeth
wheat iii quarters
malt xv busshels
which iii quarters of wheat and xv busshels of malt is delyvered into the custody of Thomas Bridge and Thomas Joselyn the newe churchwardens to be sold by
the founders commandement Summa totalis of all the recepts and charge of money
receyved by the foresaid churchewardens within the time of this their accompt as
before in the same particularly apperyth lxxiiiilbvisviiidwhereof the same churchwardens have pd within the same tyme as likewise before in the accompt apperyth
lxvilbxii8vidand so remeyneth in thands of the same churchwardens the foresaid
vithdaye of Aprill anno ixmoregni regine Elizabeth viilbxiiii" ii"1to the whiche the
same churchewardens are charged with xviilbvsoddepending upon Thomas Pechy and
Roberte Gwyn late churchewardens of foisted aforesaid viz anOvi* prioris dne regine
as appereth in their accompts of the same yere. And now the said Thomas Nevell and
Thomas Bridge do owe upon this accompt xxiiiilbxix8iid
  whereof Thomas Pechy and Robert Gwyn churchewardensof Felsted anOvitoregni
regine Elizabeth as money remayning in their hands apon the determinacion of their
accompt 7nade tlie same year xviilbvsoaThe present Thomas Novell and Thomas

Bridge nowe accompting apon this their accompt viilbxiiii8iidwhich nowe the said Thomas Nevell hath pd and delyvered apon this accompte into the hands of the said Thomas Bridge and Simon Josselyn nowe chosene churchewardens for the next yere and so the said Thomas Nevell

is quiet

Ro. Riche

per me william Bourne

Whereas Thomas Peche and Robert Gwen late churchewardens of Felsted be charged by the determinacion of this sayd last acount in the sum of xviilbvso* as by the foot of their account it doth apear of the which sayd xviilbvsodthe sayd Thomas Peche and the sayd Robert Gwen have payd by the commandement of the lord Ryche to Sir Thomas Rogerson latt chaplen of the foundation of Felsted aforesayd viiilbxsas also John thorogood and george boot latt churchewardens of Felsted aforesayd towards the wages of the usher of the said foundacion and other charges touching the sayd foundacionlband also hav payd to Thomas Bredge and Symond Jeostlen nowe beyng churchwardens of Felsted aforsayd vlbxviii8viiidand so the sayd Thomas Peche and the sayd Robert Gwen by this acount be quit descharged of the sayd xviilbvsodRo Ryche

The following notes may help to elucidate the above accounts: –

1. – The accounts have been printed as they stand, except that in a few instances abbreviations have been written in full. Thus the sign bz sometimes has been printed bushels.

2. – *Steyn lands.* – This is a farm at Moreton, still the property of the foundation.

3. – *It remeyning, etc.* – The churchwarden wrote iii"> vii8as the amount paid over by his predecessors, and made the sum total of receipts $34 3s. This was an incorrect addition for $34 5s. Robert Lord Rich, the founder's son, in auditing the accounts corrected the sum total to $34 5s.; but afterwards altered the $3 7s. and wrote xvii". It is consequently now impossible to reconcile these figures with one another.

4. – *shoten red heryngs* – i. e., herrings with the roe removed. The phrase is used by Sir John Falstaff. The word is a participle connected with vb. shoot.

5. – *pay bake.* – It is uncertain whether the former word is pay or pap – the latter might mean paper; but there is no sign of abbreviation.

6. – *foundation house.* – The house known as Ingram's stood upon the site of the house now occupied by Mr. Williams.

7. – *summa totius soluciotiis.* – The figures of the items seem to show that the amount here should be $32 6s. 8d. instead of $32 2s. 4d.

8. – S*oremaynethe*x"> ii8viiia – It is clear that the sum ought to have been $1 18s. 4d., and not $10 2s. 8d. It is probably a mere slip of the pen. The churchwarden had omitted the pence, but they were carefully added by Lord Rich.

9. – *a latteys for the come solles wyndow.* – I presume that" solle " is a variant for " soler," which means a loft, and is a word of common occurrence in old leases.

10. – *And they did sell, etc.* – The words here put in brackets have been crossed through and the rest of the account down to his signature appears to be in the hand-writing of William Bourne, Lord Rich's agent. He has added a note at the side: " Noa. To knowe whether the money is answered for the xviii bnsshels of malt."

11. – *prioris dne.* – The words are very dubious. The former is abbreviated and may be " pd," if any sense can thus bo extracted.

12. – *Bourne.* – Some words follow the signature but are too worn to be legible.

13. – The last addition to the first year's accounts seems to be wholly in the handwriting of the son and successor of Richard Lord Ryche, the founder. It is worth noting that the ink used by the churchwardens was much less lasting than my Lord's and his agent's.

14. – *Sir Thomas Bogerson.* – See page 7.

15. – *George boot.* – This is a name with which every Felstedian is familiar in its place on the remarkable house in the village.

16. – – My Lord did not enter the amount.

With slight variations, this form of rendering the accounts was maintained till 1842. In the earlier years the accounts were as a rule examined and signed by the patron. The last of these signatures is in 1623 in the form " Ro. Warwicke." It would seem, however, that the patron continued to examine the book for some years afterwards, probably till 1673. Here is a memorandum in his handwriting. " Memorandum that in this year, 1638, I did augement the scholmaster's salary to 50' and the ushers to 251. Warwicke." It will be observed that at this date the peer had conformed to the modern custom, and dropped his christiiin name in his signature. It will be seen that in the acconnts is an entry of six and eightpence paid to the vicar of Felsted. The reason for this payment is thus quaintly expressed in the accounts of a later year: – . Item pd to the vicar of Felsted for

calling uppon the churchewardens
to be mindfull of their duties in
performing the foundacion. vi" viii"

Indeed the churchwardens had other cause to be mindful. Beside the sums mentioned above they received the empty barrels withal, wherein had come the herrings, and had use of the foundation moneys, and were tardy to disgorge. Even the august patron was at length moved to wrath, and made entry in the year 1604 thus: –

Because I find great inconvenience that the accomptants detayn the stock of the foundacion in theyr hands to ther owne use, and longe time before they can be gotten to paye the same, I do order and apoint that from this time forwarde that the churchwardens shall receive no mony into their hands except they do enter into bonde to pay that which shall remain of their accompt within one month space after they have yielded their accompt.

Ro. Biche.

Divers of the earlier churchwardens had quaint views of the number that follows upon ten. Thus the officer of 1587 would seem to have ranked it with a, couple and a dozen as a word free from the formalbonds of technical arithmetic, and not to be reckoned among plebeian numerals adjectival and adhesive: –

For A leven barelles of white herrings
and A leven cadds of redd herrings xx1

A later churchwarden, varying the form of his forerunner's theory, wrote that whereof we marvel how his lips could utter the sound: –

Item pd for a eleven barrells of whit herrings.

Thereafter in diverse spelling and character is record of many labours. One summer the thatch must be renewed, and the work of two days cost fourteen pence, with ten pence to " hym that served." Then the chaplain's house needed repairing with " cley work," or dawbing, or pargetting. This last has become in modern parlance rough casting, but as a surname Pargeter still occurs. Here are three entries of work done in a later year: –

It for stoolinge a window and putting
in of three pillars Ol300d
It for stubbing and carrieing gravile 04s06*
It pd to Wesby for dobinge of walls
and strickinge of gabrills 04s00*

Windows now-a-days are rarely possessed of a stool or ledge below the sill for receipt of flower pots. The pillars may have been meant to support this, since from their cheapness they can scarce have been mullions. The mason is still said to strike a gable when he makes good any defects in its overlapping slates or tiles; but the churchwarden can hardly have known the primitive meaning of stub: else had the word not so grown in his use of it that what should have been applied onlyto the stumps of trees was made to signify the digging of gravel and clay.

In 1601 were bought sundry books for the use of the " schollers." Hereanent, if the churchwarden, anticipating later controversies, took the author of the Iliad for an impersonality and wrote of " Eustatius upon homer," at least Xenophon and Livy were known to him for men. Against the entry of " Xenophon in Greek and Latine," a later hand has written " lost." Long, too, was it ere another copy should take its place, for the time for such literary luxuries was passing away. The thrift of Elizabeth had kept words of ill omen out of the records, but with the Scotsman's accession we come nigh unto the tax. It arrived, though in other phrase, in 1612: –

Item payd unto the Kings Majestic his
officer for one payment of the enstalled
monye the fourth day of February anno
1612 10
Item payd into the King's revenue for an
acquitance 1s
It for my journey to London 3 dayes about
the paymente of the said monye 10*

It paid unto the Kings officer for the last paymente of the enstallment the 3 of February anno 1613 10lb

Much ado had the churchwardens to find wherewithal to meet their dues. The herrings must be bought and the sermon have its price, nor could the churchwardens be stinted in payment of their pains, but if the chaplain's house needed repairs he must perforce dothe work at his own charge. Happily the chaplain was Holbeach, and he had the profits of his six score scholars. When in a later year the leases fell in, he got back what moneys he had " layd out during the poverty of the foundacion." Well was it that the leases fell in, for King and Commons were in act to fall out, and here was a Puritan land that could make no stint of payment to the Parliament. Not far before did the coming taxes cast their shadows. King James' warning note had been forgotten,

when in 1638 Mr. Holbeach had his increase of salary. Gold was then plenty, and next year there was " payde to Elias Pledger a poore scholler of the schools towards his mayntenance in Cambridge by the consent of the foundation 5lb" Five years in all did Elias thus eke out his poverty, but below the fourth entry of his benevolence, as it is there called, a, re two ominous lines setting forth how the sum of $3 13s. 7d. was allowed to farm and parsonage for the subsidy. Rapidly, thereafter, the taxes rose: −
Allow'd Bromfield Parsonage for

> monthly assessments this year to
> the Parliament 07 06 09.

Hereto were added other allowances to the sum of $10 4s. 3d. The next year the work of the Association was complete. Cromwell could march northward to spend a long July evening with little content to his foes on Marston Moor, and leave his subordinates to gather money in security. This they did to the sum of $23 13s. lOd. In the year of Naseby was paid $32 16s. 8d. and in 1646, $33 4s. 5d. Six or seven shillings in the pound is no light burden, and hereby the foundationfalling into debt the churchwarden made entry thus: −

> Soe due to me upon this accompt 08 06 10.

And so remains due to this day, unless indeed my Lord saw fit to make it good, for never thereafter was mention made of the deficiency. Moreover the allowance for taxes fell behind, and goodman Gryggs, of Morton farm, perforce waited two years ere he recovered for taxes paid before 1647. In the year of Worcester fight appears the first entry for " drums and collours," which demand together with abatement for taxes continued after the Restoration. In Cromwell's latter years the taxes steadily diminished, rising once more for Charles' war with Holland and the extravagance of the Cabal. Thereafter abatements ceased, and if taxes there were the tenants alone bore the burden till they received aid for the property-tax in the last century.

Just before the Civil war the Chaplain, knowing not what should come, had thoughts, like Pisistratus:and Pericles, of beautifying his Athens: −

> For a new lanthorne at schoole and
> all chardges about it 15' 17s6d

It was a season of storms, aerial as well as political. Pepys recorded the tempest of 1661, and counted it a folly to take too much notice that thunder and lightning befel upon Coronation day. Pious Evelyn thought otherwise. In the storm of the following January he seemed to see " how exceedingly was God's hand against this ungrateful and vicious nation and court." Mr. Grlascock could scarce be surprised that his adornments did not escape scatheless, though neither diarist records this storm of 1664: −

> Item for glassinge of the schoole
> and the schoole house and the
> lanthorne of the schoole broak by
> the wind I112" 7d

Most terrible of all tempests was that which passed over pale Britannia in 1703, and to whose guidingangel, calm and serene, as he rides in the whirlwind and directs the storm, Addison likened the hero of Blenheim. Twice over has Mr. Lydiatt made record of this storm: −

Novemb. 26, 27, 1703, raged so dreadfull a tempest, so distructive both by Land and Sea that History scarce records a greater. The Lanthorn of the Schole was blown down and much damage done to the foundation buildings.

Well for Mr. Lydiatt that the storm was not in school hours. Else might his fate have been as Bishop Kidder's, once vicar of Rayue, and thereafter supplanter of the gentle Ken, then resting in the shades of Longleat. The bishop and his wife were slain both of them. by a falling chimney in his palace at Wells. Though thus everted the lantern survived to be set anew with brick and tile and crowned with a vane, whose cost was thirteen shillings and nine pence.

But let us return and regard the bill for a pigsty or sheepcote (who shall say which?) building, while Charles the second was saddening Evelyn as aforesaid: –

It pd Mr. Idle for straw to thatch a
hoggs coate 00 02 00
It to Cooke for thatchinge it 00 02 06
It pd Chandler for 300 of nayles to
board it 00 01 0(i
It for nayles to lath it 00 00 03
It for 2 rasons and spurrs for the same 00 01 06.

Rasons are the timbers whereto are fastened the bottoms of the rafters and spurs the buttresses thereabove. In the same season the almsfolk had sundry repairs. The frame of a posnett,*i. e.*little pot, cost sixpence to the foundation and a new skillet five and eightpence. Here also are two terms extinct with the extinction hereabouts of the industry to which they refer. A cheese " moate " is the wooden or wicker vessel that gives its shape to the cheese. A "pealle" is a source of contention, but may haply be the board whereon the cheeses are afterwards placed. Our churchwarden knows also the modern peel that is used by the baker.

In 1710 the old book was full, and Mr. Lydiatt ordered a new volume and decked it with the founder's arms. Herein he entered, not always with accuracy, what he deemed of moment in the older records. Not much did Mr. Lydiatt deem of moment, and when he varies the phrase it is not always for the better. Bead the fate of the poor usher as Mr. Lydiatt gives it: –

1626. In this year Mr. Raymond had his quietus being superannuated but had his sallary of 10lbcontinued to 1637.

The unconscious irony of the older record has merely " to Mr. Raymond for his benevolence." Mr. Lydiatt-with daring prophecy records in 1707 how in this year " was begun the annual meeting of the gentlemen educated in this schole," how Sir Charles Harringtonand Martin Carter were stewards, how there was an entertainment in the school, and how he, the said Simon Lydiatt, M. A., was preacher, and took for his text St. Paul's quotation from the Greek poets. " Printed " wrote also Mr. Lydiatt in a note at the side. A patriot, too, was the worthy chaplain, following the daring deeds of his time, and in 1709 setting as a theme for a Latin oration " Gallis non fidendum." Whereof he adds explanation for the use of posterity: "In this year France sued for peace but flew off from the preliminarys." Moreover it is written how "Th6m. Lydiat setat 15" won the prize and delivered the oration. It was the year of Malplaquet, and next July son or nephew Thomas orated again on the theme of " Triumphus melior pace."

Here is an entry made by Mr. Hutchin: – March the 14th, 1719. N. B. – One widow Calwald, from London, brought his Lordship's order to be admitted into the almshouse in the room of widow Gilbert, deceased, but upon hearing the articles read to her would not accept of it, and so after 3 or 4 days spent here returned to London. And thus derided by Mr. Chaplain for a whimsical cockney, widow Calwald made room for widow Poole of Bromefield, a less wealthy or less exacting dame. Again who shall say what tragedy of poverty may be behind these two entries for 1722: –

Received from old Bailey's goods $1 0s6d

Pd for old Bailey's buriall 4s4*

And of old Bailey neither before nor after beside thisis any word. Haply he was the man who received now and again scant pittance for " swanging" the pastures, that is to say mowing down thistles, and uprooting weeds from marshy spots. Here again is unconscious irony in the payment of a few shillings for the mending of seventy-seven quarrels. Were they of man with man, the price were little; but in truth these quarrels were made of glass, diamonds thereof set in lead, and the price paid for putting other quarrels in their place. Once more here is a strange entry little older than a century: –

Wm. Joyce for throwing of mud 10s6d

Nowadays the operation is sometimes performed gratis, though haply the throwers look for some reward. And so with the old refrain of herrings, and ever herrings, our record comes down to the memory of living man.

THE HOUSE OP RICH.

| HE origin of the family of Lord Rich has been matter of some discussion. On the whole it seems best to accept the statement of Philpot that the cradle of the race was in Hampshire. The first of the family of whom there is definite information was Richard Rich, a wealthy mercer of London and Sheriff of the City in 1441. The date of his death is given by Burke as 1469, but it would seem that he has been confounded with his son John, who was buried in the Mercer's chapel in that year. The family remained in the city, and the son of John Rich was probably also a mercer. To him was born sometime between 1480 and 1490 a son whom he named Richard. As the boy grew up he showed that he had a soul which, whether above or below commerce, was at any rate alien from it. His father, foreseeing that, if his son were his partner, the profits of the business were likely to disappear in the gaminghouses of Whitefriars, gave the youth his wish and let him study the common law. At the Middle Temple, though his reading was

neither I nor any man else to my knowledge ever took you to be a man of such credit as either I or any other would vouchsafe to communicate with you in any matter of importance?" However, the evidence, backed by the summing up of the presiding judge, was enough to secure a verdict in that court. How far Rich was consciously dishonest is a question which may be left undecided. In 1537 Cromwell wanted a man to manage the Commons in the matter of dissolving the larger monasteries. It was a year of discontents and insurrections, but the King and his minister were not to be turned from their purpose. The rooks had been harried, but now at all hazards the rookeries were to be demolished. A timid man would have dreaded the possibilities of the future, but cowardice was not one of the faults of Richard Rich. He accepted his election as Speaker of the Commons and performed with great skill the task that he had undertaken. He was placed at the head of the Court of Augmentations, the commission appointed to carry out the dissolution of the monasteries. The grants of their lands passed through his hands, and it was, in Fuller's phrase, no wonder if some stuck upon his fingers. Some of his family had already purchased property in Essex, and it was in this county that he established himself. Something like a hundred manors, including Leez Priory with its three parks, was perhaps no inadequate reward for his services. It is difficult to say how many of them were direct grants from the crown. Probably a large part of his other savings went in building the stately mansion that was destined to be for five generations the home of his descendants. We cannot hei-e omit the story that Rich, with his own hands, turned the screw of the rack on Anne Askew, but the evidence for it is by no means certain.

In the latter years of Henry's reign Rich attached himself closely to the relatives of the heir apparent. The King himself, as his strength failed, naturally affected the same party, and Rich was named 111 Henry's will as one of the sixteen executors of the kingdom during Edward's minority. It was the prelude to the grant of the Great Seal. In 1547 an intrigue ousted Wriothesley, and Rich, who just before had been one of a batch of new barons, so exposed the incompetently of Paulet that in October he was himself appointed to the Lord Chancellorship of England.

In spite of the idleness of his youth there can be little doubt that he was fully competent to perform the duties of his office and that he did so with satisfaction to the public. For more than four years he despatched alone the whole business of the court. He had meantime to steer a difficult course amid the factions of the time.

The first trouble that arose was the quarrel between Somerset and his brother, Lord Seymour of Sudeley. On no ground was Lord Rich likely to assist the younger brother. Of the bill of attainder which was brought in against Lord Seymour the Lord Chancellor had the charge. Although the great majority of both houses were ready to vote for the bill, Lord Rich took care to fortify himself with the opinion of the Judges and the Council. On receiving a guarded statementthat some of the charges amounted to treason he proceeded with the bill and afterwards signed the warrant for the execution. In the contention between Somerset and Dudley, Lord Rich, after some hesitation, threw in his lot with the latter. It*in*assumed that he had none but personal motives in the matter. It is, however, possible that he may have possessed the knowledge that Dudley, like himself, was at heart no friend of the reformed doctrines. Whatever his motives may have been, he was able to do good service to his ambitious leader. As a Londoner by birth, the son of one leading merchant and the son-in-law of another, he had nolittle influence in the City. To the leaders of the City in Council assembled he set forth, in a powerful harangue, what were accounted the misdeeds of the Protector. The punishment of Somerset was much less severe than might have been expected, and it is. not impossible that Lord Rich may have purposely taken so leading a part against him in order to mitigate the severity of his fall. Such a view is not inconsistent with either of the two accounts of his subsequent conduct.

A difficulty remains in regard to the Chancellor's conduct towards the Princess Mary. Dudley, now created Duke of Northumberland, was ostensibly carrying on the

work of the Reformation, and the measures taken against the Princess were largely
entrusted to the conduct of Lord Rich. If he was really as harsh in carrying them out
as all the evidence seems to show, how is it that he was again entrusted with local
executive powers when the Princess came to>the throne? Perhaps the Queen could
not afford to discard any who were likely to be serviceable in the work there was to
do.

The retirement of Lord Rich coincides with the last quarrel between Somerset and
Northumberland. Of the circumstances which led to it two accounts are given. On the
one hand it is said that when Somerset, always popular with the poor of the nation,
seemed 4o have good hopes of regaining his influence, the 'Chancellor, seeing that he
had in any case much to lose and little to gain, determined to retire of his own accord.
** Like a skilful pilot, who, seeing a storm at Tiand, gets his ship into harbour, he
made suit to the King by reason of some bodily infirmities that he might be discharged
of his office." His great wealth and length of days make this story plausible, and it
would be pleasant to accept it. There is, however, better evidence for another account.
According to this Rich, perceiving how Somerset was again rising to power, began
again to court his favour. Even when Somerset had been betrayed and sent to the
Tower there was a chance that his popularity might yet avail him. Lord Rich was
therefore anxious to serve him, and sent a letter to the Tower to warn him of some
design that Warwick had against him. He directed his letter in such haste that it was
addressed merely " To the Duke." The Duke of Norfolk was also in the Tower,. and
the servant who tore the letter, knowing his master's acquaintance with Norfolk, and
ignorant of his renewed communication with Somerset, handed the letter to the wrong
Duke. Lord Rich heard of the mistake in time. He took to his bed and wrote to the
King to say that he was exceeding sick and must resign the Great Seal forthwith: let
officers be sent to fetch it, for he was too weak to move. The device saved him and
he retired in peace to Leez. It may be observed that it is possible to accept the facts
of this story without admitting the motives ascribed to the Chancellor. Somerset was
already arrested when Rich wrote to him, and the letter may have been due to so good
a motive as the desire to help an old friend and colleaguein the hour of his need.

At Leez Lord Rich lived in retirement till the death of the King. The accession of
Mary found more work for the old man. Largely as he had been enriched by the spoil
of the monasteries, closely as he had been connected with the reforming measures of
Somerset, he had remained in doctrine an adherent of the Papacy. No sooner was the
old order restored than he hastened to establish at Felsted masses for the repose of
the dead. In the persecutions and martyrdoms which followed he had unfortunately
no little part. Protestant feeling was as strong in Essex as in any part of the kingdom,
and not a few of the victims of that sad time were condemned by Lord Rich and his
colleagues. So strong was the odium cast upon them that some of them quailed before
it, and endeavoured to throw the responsibility upon the Council. The Council, in their
turn, were naturally unwilling to bear the whole burden, and wrote sharp directions to
Lord Rich to act upon his own responsibility. When, in consequence, the number of
burnings diminished, Lord Rich againreceived a strong order to bring more heretics
to the stake. Happily, the fires were not to last much longer,. and with the accession
of Elizabeth the public life of Lord Rich came to an end.

Of his private life little is known beyond genealogical facts. Before he rose to eminence he married Elizabeth, daughter of Thomas Jenks, a member of the Grocers' Company. Her brother William was a member of the same company. By her Lord Rich had a family of four sons and nine daughters. Of the descendants of his daughters some account is given below. Of his sons three died young, and one of them, Thomas, had sepulture at Felsted, where there is a brass to his memory in the church. Lord Rich died at Rochford, 12th June, 1567, at the age of about four score years. His body was brought in stately procession from Rochford to Leez, and thence to Felsted, where a monument was erected to his memory. The recumbent figure of the Chancellor is most characteristic. The small head and keen features mark the skill of the lawyer and the wariness of the statesman. The gilt and paint of the monument have almost disappeared, while the loss of the original inscriptions is ill compensated by the defacement of impertinent initials. Below is a brass to Lord Rich's grandson, the first of the race to find sepulture at Felsted. The diglottic inscription marks the need of Felsted School. " Thomas Ryche filius Roberti Ryche militis obiit 1564 et sepultus est apud Felsted the 4th of Februarye."

Robert, second Lord Rich, was thirty years of age when he succeeded to the title. Unlike his father, ho

ungrudgingly accepted the doctrines of the Reforma. tion, and without taking a very prominent part, made some figure in the court of Elizabeth. On the trial of the fourth Duke of Norfolk, for his part in the Ridolfi plot, Lord Rich sat as one of the judging peers, and was employed in different diplomatic negotiations by the Queen. He seems to have been a good man of business, attending carefully to his own property and to the management of the Felsted foundation. By his wife, Elizabeth, daughter of George Baldry, he had a large family, as set forth in the pedigree given at the end of Chapter IV. His eldest son died without issue in 1580, and he himself in the following year. He was succeeded by his eldest surviving son Robert. This third Lord was, perhaps, the first of the family in whom appeared those Puritan views which were characteristic of its most famous members. He married in 1580 the sister of Elizabeth's later favourite, the second Earl of Essex, nnd was associated with his brother-in-law in most of his successes, and in the disastrous close of his career. He was with Essex in 1596, when the English squadron sailed to Cadiz, burnt the Spanish fleet, and captured the town. In the following year he accompanied Essex to Ireland, but took no part in the treason which brought the impetuous Earl to the block. Before these events Lord Rich's married life had come to a disastrous pass. The marriage was not the result of affection, at any rate on the side of Lady Penelope Devereux. She was but twenty at the time, and had already fallen in love with Sir Philip Sidney. Sidney's prospects were clouded by the fall of his patron, Leicester, in 1580.

Lady Penelope's relations found a more promising
match in the heir of the house of Rich, and when
Sidney returned to court his mistress was another's.
He gave vent to his feelings in a bitter dirge: –
" Prom so ungrateful fancy,
From such a female frenzy,
Prom them that use men thus,

Good Lord, deliver us! "

He found only too soon that his mistress's heart had not gone with her hand, and addressed to her the tsonnets which after his death were published as Astrophel and Stella.*In*truth there could be little. sympathy between the gay Stella and her stern, perhaps violent, husband. Sidney's marriage in 1583 put an end to the liaison, but Lady Rich soon found another to fill his place. Her husband had forgiven frer former conduct, but in 1590 she openly transferred lier affections to the brilliant bat unprincipled Lord Mountjoy. Even then her husband was unwilling to take extreme steps, and it was not until 1601 that he finally separated from her. A divorce followed and. she immediately married Mountjoy. Laud forgot his principles and performed the ceremony, a fact often remembered against him when he had risen to greatness. For these events it has been usual to lay the larger part of the blame upon Lord Rich. The charge is really unjust. The poets of the time were not tho men to judge fairly between a stern Puritan and such courtiers as Mountjoy and Sidney, while later writers have been so dazzled by the picturesque career of the hero of Zutphen that they have had no eyes for his sin. Lord Rich's sons bore ample testimony to the integrity of their father's life and the godliness of his household. Nor can their evidence be gainsaid by the partisan sneers of Clarendon, who after all could do little more than adduce the undisputed fact that Lady Rich was unfaithful to her husband. Lord Rich took to his third wife Frances, daughter of Sir Christopher Wray, who outlived him twenty years.

In his later years Lord Rich took little part in public life. In 1618 he received from King James a patent of the Earldom of Warwick. He had no local connexion willi that town, but chose for its past glories a title which had been borne by Beauchamps, Nevilles, Plantagenets, and Dudleys. It has been suggested, though there is no evidence on the point, that hebought his new honours of the penurious King. Be that as it may, he did not enjoy them long. Dying in the same year, he was succeeded by his eldest son, Robert, second Earl of Warwick and fourth Lord Rich of Leez.

' So far as the present writer is aware, no life of the greatest of the Rich family has yet been written. The second Earl of Warwick of this creation was born in 1587, and married before his father's death, Frances, daughter of Sir William Hatton. He inherited the large estates in Essex, and with them the patronage of the Felsted School and Charities. It would, however, seem probable that there was a large debt on the estate,. accumulated perhaps by his father and grandfather,. who found no light cost in the court of Elizabeth. This debt, no less than his sympathy with Puritanical

views, may have been the reason why Lord Warwick eschewed the court. Instead of loitering away life in the frivolities of Whitehall he employed his younger years in settling colonies in the West Indies. He had a grant of land on the continent of America as well as a large share in the Bermudas, which had been colonised by Somers in 1609. Waller says of a battle with twowhales, left by the tide in a lagoon in the Bermudas. that it took place

" Within the bounds of noble Warwick's share: Warwick's bold Earl, than which no title bears A greater sound among our British peers."

Warwick made several voyages to the still-vext Bermoothes, and that part of the islands where his property lay was long called after his name. It may be surmised that it was rather by the profits of these plantations than, as has been insinuated, by the plunder of the civil war, that he freed his property from debt. At any rate as early as 1640 his English estates were held to be worth more than seven thousand a year, a large income in those days, and there is no mention of iucumbrauces. After the accession of Charles I. Warwick began to take a more prominent part in public life. His voyages on the Atlantic had turned his attention to naval affairs. As a Puritan he deeply sympathised with the attempts of the unfortunate Elector Palatine to recover his position and power. He did his best to assist both him and the Prince of Orange, and was present at the Prince's capture of Breda in 1637. On his return he was caught by a tempest and saved only by his skill as a sailor.

During the years when the King was governing without a Parliament, Warwick's wealth and abilities and his close connexion with Lord Kimbolton gave him a leading place in the Presbyterian party. His house and his purse were opened to the ministers who had been silenced and deprived by the illegal courts. At the same time he was no bitter enemy of episcopacy, and at the beginning of the Long Parliament would seem to have been in favour of milder courses than commended themselves even to Falkland. He concurred, however, in the prosecution of Strafford and Laud. When in 1642 the King revoked Northumberland's commission as Lord High Admiral, Warwick, who was already ViceAdmiral, was appointed by the Parliament to fill his place. He had long been a friend of Cromwell's, and the friendship stood the test of some difference in political views. For the present the Earl and Cromwell were acting in complete accord, and on the King's declaration of war Warwick secured the navy for the cause of the Parliament. Only two captains refused to follow him, and they were straightway sent-prisoners to the Parliament. Warwick's activity at this crisis was of immense. service to the Parliament and the country. Had Pennington and Mennes met with any success in their attempt to establish a Royalist party in the fleet, it is probable that a cival war by sea would have aggravated the horrors of the time. As it was, the fleet, without taking a very active part in the war, succeeded in effectually protecting the commerce of the country. A squadron was annually equipped under Warwick's. superintendence and occasionally took the offensive.

Warwick assisted in the pitiful discomfiture of Prince Maurice at Lyme Regis, but was wholly unsuccessful i u relieving Exeter in 1643. In that year Warwick, with his sons-in-law, Robartes and Manchester, was of the two and twenty peers who sat in Parliament. Meantime his great influence in Essex was used in the c-ause of the Association, and ho found time to take part in the ordinary government of the county. Thus in July 1640 we find him listening to a sermon at Chelmsford, and therefrom proceeding to the trial of eighteen women on an accusation of witchcraft. Warwick's steward, Arthur Wilson, whose body lies in the chancel of Felsted church, records that to him they seemed not witches but merely " poore, melanchollio, envious, mischevous, ill-disposed, ill-dieted, atrabilus constitutions." Warwick was more superstitious than his servant, and the women were all executed.

It is not very easy to trace Warwick's course during the involved negociations which followed the civil war. For a time he certainly continued to act with the moderate Presbyterians. When the King was at Holmby early in 1647, Warwick was of the party that was anxious to come to an agreement with him. When in the following May the Parliament made an attempt to disband the army, Warwick was one of the commissioners sent down for that purpose to Newmarket. On the failure of the attempt he returned to London, and remained there till July '26th. On that day the apprentices of the city, with a turbulent mob, broke into the Parliament house, and compelled the Commons to recall eleven Presbyterian members whohad been dismissed six weeks before. It would seem that Warwick had small sympathy with the extreme Presbyterians, and from this time he acted more closely with the Independents. As a protest against the violence of the City mob he withdrew, with the Speaker. and most of the Independent members, to the protection of the army. It has been represented that his object in so doing was to have a share in any treaty which the army might be making with the King. But in fact there were many motives to draw him towards the army. He was on intimate terms with Cromwell, and Cromwell had begun to doubt the King's sincerity, and to fall in with the views of the mass of the soldiery. Almost alone among the Presbyterians, Warwick was no less a soldier than a politician, and the methods of the Presbyterians can at no time have greatly commended themselves to his judgment. If the Presbyterians were to be controlled by the fatuous turbulence of the city mob, there could be no place for him among them. The question remains, what part he took in the Royalist reaction of the following winter. The leaders of the Presbyterians were on the sido of the King. Warwick's brother, Lord Holland, actually rose in arms, and Clarendon asserts that Warwick himself secretly assisted the movement. Without himself appearing on that side, he is alleged to have sent a dependent, one Colonel Farr, to raise troops in Essex. The statement, if true, involves a charge of cowardice, but it is almost demonstrably false. The motive assigned by Clarendon is mere pique. The command of the fleet had been transferred from Warwick to Rainsborough, an extremeIndependent, but the fleet, always Presbyterian, had refused to receive its new commander, and was using its power on the side of the Parliament. Now if Warwick had really wished to oppose the Independents, there was nothing to prevent his taking advantage of this feeling of the seamen and putting himself at their head for the cause of the King. He did go down to Portsmouth, but that his object was not to assist the rising is shewn by the boast of Evelyn that the*Rich*was sent empty away. Evelyn further declares that he was not likely to be received by the fleet unless he changed his spots and avowed their protestations. In the second place, we have Arthur Wilson's account of what actually took place at Leez. Wilson was in his master's confidence; and, if he had received orders to give secret aid to the movement, nothing would have been easier than to make a show of resistance to the Royalists, and allow them to carry off arms and stores from Leez. On the contrary, when Goring, who commanded the rising in Essex, sent word to Wilson that he was coming to dine at Leez and would " borrow my lord's arms," Wilson did his best to conceal the arms. He boastfully relates his success in outwitting Goring, who went away with far fewer arms than he had reason to expect. Finally Clarendon's accusation is wholly inconsistent with Warwick's conduct when he resumed the command of the fleet, and with the earnest efforts which he subsequently made to save his brother's life. Had he been coward enough to support his brother in secret, while he disavowed him openly, he would scarcely have used all his influence on the side of mercy

In the autumn of 1648 Warwick was again in command of the navy. Like its commander, the fleet was losing faith in the Presbyterian policy, and, with Warwick at its head, lay opposed to Prince Rupert off the coast of Holland. Some dubious negociations took place between them, and Warwick was accused of a design to coalesce with the Prince. His answer to the charge is consistent with all his conduct, and has an uninistakeable ring of sincerity. " As to the pretended

resolution of my joining with the Prince

I do profess in the presence of God, who knows my heart and ways, that it never entered into my thoughts, and that my soul abhors it as inconsistent with my duty, prejudicial to the Parliament, destructive to the kingdom's peace, and unworthy of a free-born Englishman." In fact Warwick was not treacherous, but was skilfully following the tactics of Fabius. Evelyn soon afterwards told his father-in-law that his aim had been to tire out the enemy with overwatching, and many years later Sir William Batten gave the same account to Pepys. In the subsequent winter Warwick was again in London, and, to the surprise of some, came in to the Agreement of the people, by which the King's rights were expressly ignored. Though, however, he had thus definitely broken with the Presbyterians, he was not prepared to recognise the sole authority of the House of Commons, or take any part in the measure* against the King's life. He continued to support the government as established by the Agreement, and afterwards helped to invest Cromwell with the purple robe, but he was not satisfied with the constitution of the Protector's parliaments, and was unwilling to take part in their deliberations. This difference of opinion caused no loss of friendship, and both Warwick and Cromwell were active in 1657 in bringing about a marriage between the Earl's grandson, Robert, and Frances, the Protector's youngest daughter. The marriage took place in November, but the bridegroom's death in the following February broke the old Earl's heart. He went down to Leez for the funeral, and when it was delayed longer than he expected, he was heard to say, " if they stayed a little longer they should carry him down to be buried with him." Two months later, April 18th, 1658, the old man was gathered to his fathers. Cromwell, who had written brave words of encouragement to his old friend and been nobly answered, never recovered from the blow.

Clarendon and some lesser authorities have passed unfavourable judgment on Warwick's character. Unable to deny his influence over men whose uprightness could not be gainsaid, they have accused him of studied hypocrisy and a concealment of libertinism under the cloak of listening to long sermons. Clarendon goes so far as to say that a man of less virtue could not be found. For this accusation it would seem that there is really no ground. It was Clarendon's business to write down his opponents, and no man had done better service for the cause of the Parliament than Warwick. A more impartial view of his character would show that he was an honest man, equally averse to tyranny and to anarchy. His sympathies were in many ways with the Presbyterians, but they were tempered by the love of

order and the spirit of toleration. In no other way does it seem possible to account for all his actions. In fact we shall find no reason to quarrel with the eulogy which Edmund Calamy uttered over his grave: "All who knew him loved him, and if any man did not love him, 'twas because he did not know him."

Warwick had four sons, two of whom died young, and three daughters. His eldest son, Robert, married Anne, daughter of the Earl of Devonshire, and their only child married Frances Cromwell. Lady Rich died at Leez in 1638, lamented by all who knew her. Little Sidney Godolphin, himself destined to fall in his prime, fighting ex parte regis, found food for his natural melancholy in mourning for so heavy a loss: – " Possess'd of all that nature could bestow, All we can wish to be or reach to know, Equal to all the patterns which our mind Can frame of good beyond the good we find." In verse perhaps not equally sincere, Waller imprecated for Leez something like the fate that has befallen it: – " May those already curst Essexian plains, Where hasty death and pining sickness reigns,. Prove all a desert, and none there make stay But savage beasts or men as wild as they." Indeed, it was a curious fatality that impelled the house of Rich to live amid the malarious fishponds of Leez and have their place of burial on the healthy height of Felsted. Lord Rich sought consolation in a second wife, a daughter of Sir Thomas Cheeke, of Pirgo, by whom he had three daughters, the second of whom became the mother of Bolingbroke. He seems to have been a worthless libertine, though in the civil war he opposed his father and was with the King at Oxford. Even his gentle cousin, Dorothy Osborn, called him a man of small honour. He was one of those who in June 1642 signed the unfortunate declaration that the King had no intention of war. In July he, with eight others, was impeached by the Commons and declared incapable of sitting and voting during that Parliament. This judgment was not repealed till after the Restoration, when Rich was dead. During the Commonwealth his father's influence and his lack of separate property protected him from all unpleasantness. For hia son's marriage with Frances Cromwell he naturally had little liking, but he did not decline to be present at the ceremony. It would have made little difference if he had. He died in, 1659, and was succeeded by his brother Charles. This Earl was one of the committee that was sent by Parliament in 1660 to wait upon Charles II. at the Hague. On his return he seems to have lived in gouty retirement at Leez till his death in 1673. He had enough Puritan leaven to turn his back in disgust upon the scandals of the Court. By his wife, a daughter of the great Earl of Cork, he had an only son, who died before him. The widowed and childless Countess continued to reside at Leez, and had such consolation as might be found in works of charity. She seems to have fully earned the title which was given to her funeral sermon, " The virtuous woman found." Dr. Walker, of Fyfield, had before celebrated in like sort her son and her husband. To his sermons, entitled " Planctus Unigeniti" andi'Leez lachrymans," he now in 1678added the " Heureka." Lady Warwick was a sister of Robert Boyle, and showed her kinship in the shape of her nose.

We must now return to Henry, younger son of the first Earl of Warwick. The condition of the familyestate made it necessary for the young man to carve out a fortune for himself. As a lad he served as a volunteer in Holland, and returning to spend a winter in England, attracted by his good looks the attention of King James. More than twenty years later the poet could speak of his comeliness in such terms as these: – " Thy beauty, too, exceeds the sex of men; Thy courtly presence and thy princely grace Add to the splendor of thy royal race." Those were perilous times, and young Rich showed his tact by attaching himself to the Duke of Buckingham and seeming desirous of obtaining the royal favour only by means of the favourite. The King lavished great sums upon the handsome courtier, and used his prerogative to marry him to the heiress of Sir Walter Cope, of Kensington, who had built there the palace which he called Cope Castle. Accordingly Tickell is mistaken in saying of that house that it was

" Rear'd by bold chiefs of Warwick's noble race." However, the wings and arcades, one of the chief beauties of the house, were added by Lord Holland. On one occasion, when Rich and another courtier were with the King, there passed through the room an officer of the Treasury with a bag of three thousand sovereigns in his hand. " How happy that money would make me," whispered Rich to his companion. TheKing heard what he had said, and ordered the money to be given him. Altogether it is said that a hundred and fifty thousand pounds was received by Rich from the King. Moreover, he was created in. 1622 Baron Kensington, and in 1624 Earl of Holland. Thereupon he renamed his wife's mansion Holland House, the title which it still bears. On the negotiation for the marriage of Prince Charles with Henrietta Maria, Lord Holland was sent as ambassador to France, and so won the Princess's favour that in after days idle rumours floated about the English Court. For years he remained a courtier and on intimate terms with the Queen, but was no friend to her husband's ministers. Strafford once said, foolishly enough, that the King would do well to cut off Holland's head. Holland did not forget this expression of opinion. In the expedition against Scotland in 1639 he had the command of the horse, and his retreat from Dunse was much and unjustly criticised. A quarrel with Newcastle followed. The King prevented a duel, and it was thought that Holland had let Charles know what was doing. On. the outbreak of the civil war Holland sided with the Parliament, which had already employed him to carry the petition to the King at Beverley. However, he soon wearied of a war in which he had nothing to gain. In 1643 he deserted the Parliament and made his way to Oxford, where he was somewhat coldly received by the King and Queen. He seems to have thought that the past would be wholly ignored; and when he found that even great courage shown at Newbury was but faintly commended, and that there was no hope ofrestoration to his offices, he returned to the army of the Parliament. There he was thoroughly mistrusted and for a time thrown into prison. His own plea was that he had striven to act as a mediator. When the breach between Presbyterians and Independents became manifest, he plotted a rising in the King's favour. The whole affair was grossly mismanaged. Holland collected a small force at Kingston-on-Thames, where he allowed himself to be surprised by a small Parliamentary force. He took to flight with a hundred horsemen, and wandered about without aim or purpose till he was taken prisoner at St. Neot's. He was brought to trial, with Hamilton and others, condemned, and executed on March 9th, 1649.

It is hard to find anything to admire in the character of Lord Holland. He was in spirit an adventurer, and though there was something genuine in his Presbyterianism, his vacillations during the war were due to his doubt which side was likely to be victorious. In his last rising he showed neither courage nor judgment, and it is impossible to deny that he deserved his fate.

None of Holland's four sons made any figure in the world, and the most famous of his daughters was of tarnished fame. She loved too well the Duke of Ormonde, but married Sir James Thynne, " a wealthy beast," and lived as unhappily as she deserved. Her youngest sister, Diana, who never married, was of very different character. She was an intimate friend of her cousin, Dorothy Osborn, who says that her beauty was the least of her excellences. Moreover, we have it on her own testimony that she was "a friend to thetobacco-box." Lord 'Holland's eldest son Robert succeeded him in the Earldom, and on the death of his cousin in 1673, succeeded also to the Earldom of Warwick and the Barony of Rich of Leez. Little is known of the Earl except that he was active with Lady Devonshire in the cause of the Restoration. His eldest surviving son Edward, who succeeded him in his titles and estates, was a man of loose principles and profligate life. He was a friend of Lord Mohun and all the Scourers and Mohocks of those lawless days. For his share in a discreditable brawl, in which his friend Captain Coote was stabbed, he was in 1699 brought t6trial for his life. Lord Warwick, with Mohun, Coote, and three others had been drinking at the Greyhound in the Strand. As they passed through the bar at an early hour in the morning a squabble arose and swords were drawn. The evidence at the trial was somewhat conflicting, but there could be no doubt that chairs were ordered and the company was carried to Leicester Square. The chairmen were dismissed, but almost immediately recalled, to find Coote dying of two grievous wounds, another of the company badly hurt, <ind no blood on any sword but Lord Warwick's. Lord Warwick's story was that the fight had been between Coote and Janes, the wounded man, while he himself,. going to succour Coote, had been badly wounded in the hand. The House of Lords, with Lord Somers as Lord High Steward, refused to believe this account, and though they acquitted him of the capital charge, found him guilty of manslaughter on their honour. He claimed his clergy, and was dismissed with a cautionfrom Somers. Two years afterwards he died, and his widow was afterwards married to Addison. His only son and successor in the title was that Earl to whom,. according to some accounts, Addison was tutor when he fell in love with the Countess Dowager. There is no real proof that Addison filled such an office, but twocharming letters from him to the young Earl are not inconsistent with the account. If we may judge from Lord Warwick's epitaph in Kensington Church, he wasa model of all excellences and " propriis quam majorum virtutibus clarior." It is more usual to believe that hewas a worthless young profligate whom Addison strove to reclaim, and who repaid him by bearing idle tales to Pope. These are said to have provoked Pope's bitterlines on Atticus. It is reported, perhaps falsely, that Addison on his deathbed sent for his step-son to show him how a Christian could die: – " He taught us how to live, and (oh, too high

The price for knowledge!) taught us how to die." We may prefer to think that the Earl's faults have been exaggerated in order to give special point to a couplet. There can be no doubt that Addison loved the youth,. and that Tickell heartily prayed for his prosperity: – " Let manly constancy confirm his truth

And gentlest manners crown his blooming youth." Macaulay holds that his blooming youth preferred such display of manners as might be made by " rolling women in hogsheads down Holborn-hill." For such or for nobler amusements he had little more opportunity. Two years later the same poet told how

" Short-liv'd Warwick sadden'd all the shades."

There is an unhappy ambiguity in the line, for if the Earl was all that his detractors have painted him, respectable shades may well have shown little pleasure at his presence in the Elysian fields.

The Earl's property went to his aunt, the ancestress of the present Lord Kensington, and his titles descended to his second cousin, Edward, eighth Earl of Warwick, fifth Earl of Holland, and tenth Baron Rich of Leez. The last Earl seems to have had none of the family property save the living of St. Bartholomew the Great, in Smithfield, and perhaps Warwick House. He took no great part in public affairs, bat occasionally appeared in his place in the House of Lords, as at the trial of Lord Lovat, in 1746. He was so little known that the Annual Register for 1759 does not even notice his death. From the fact that he was among the subscribers to Burnet's " History of his own Times," would it be rash to infer that he was either a man of literary tastes, or a Whig, or both? His Countess survived him ten years. Their only daughter, Lady Charlotte Rich, was born in 1713, died in Queen Anne Street, in April, 1791, and had sepulture with her ancestors in the vault at Kensington. She was the last of her house, and probably the death's-head took the place of the knot on the lozenge of her maiden hatchment: –

" Grass of Levitie, Span in Brevitie,
Wind's Stabilitie, is Mortalitie."

It would be an endless task to trace all the descendants of Lord Rich in the female lines. At the presenttime there are at least seventy peers of the realm and many thousand commoners who have his blood in their veins. A few of his descendants may be mentioned. From his third daughter, Dorothy, sprang the Osborns, baronets of Chicksands. Of this house were Sir Peter 'Osborn, the gallant defender of Guernsey in the civil war, and his daughter Dorothy, who married Sir William Temple. Her charming letters to her lover have of late been widely read. Sir William had a large family, whereof one only lived to maturity. This was his son John, who was engaged in Irish affairs for William III. His failure therein so preyed upon his mind that he drowned himself under Westminster Bridge. Of John Temple's two daughters, one married her cousin, a man of whom Sheldon said that he had the curse of the gospel, for that all men spake well of him. From Winifred Lady North descends the house of North, Barons North of Kirtling, and Earls of Guilford. Of the descendants of Lady Darcy, Lord Rich's youngest daughter, are living a multitude, which includes nearly a twelfth part of the present House of Lords. General Gage, who held the command against Washington, was of this line. Lady Darcy's granddaughter Penelope was a lady of much beauty and a pretty wit. Three suitors quarrelled for her hand, whereon she threatened with her everlasting displeasure him who should first show violence. Let them possess their souls in patience, and she would choose one forthwith and marry the others as occasion served. Sir George Trenchard was the favoured suitor, but the lady lived to fulfil her promise, and Sir John Gage andSir William Harvey in succession claimed and obtained lier hand.

From Sir Edwin Rich sprang the baronets of that name, seated at Mulbarton, in Norfolk. The ultimate heiress of this line married a Bostock, who adopted the name and arms of his wife. The baronetcy was revived in his favour, and is now held by his great-grandson, Sir C. H. S. Rich. From Lady Essex Cheeke are descended many noble lines. Lord Lake, the hero of the Mahratta war, was the grandson of her grandson. The Countess of Manchester is directly represented by the Duke of Manchester, and in the female line by many other peers. From Lady Robartes is sprung the present Lord

Robartes. The line of her niece, Lady Mary St. John, became extinct on the death of Henry, Lord Bolingbroke, in 1751. Among the many descendants of the Countess of Nottingham, one has married a daughter of Queen Victoria. From the youngest daughter of the first Earl of Holland is sprung a numerous host. She was represented at Waterloo by the gallant Earl of Uxbridge, afterwards Marquis of Anglesey. From Lady Elizabeth Edwardes, daughter of the fifth Earl of Warwick, descends Lord Kensington, in favour of whose great-grandfather that title was revived. He is at present the nearest representative of the main line of Lord Rich, from whom he is ninth in descent.

Something has already been said of the part played by the Riches under the house of Stuart. Many of their descendants gathered also to the court of George [. and his son. There, for a moment, was the greatest of them all, Heniy St. John Viscount Bolingbroke, bowing "three times down to the very gronnd," when he did homage to the King, and leaving his presence to plot his ruin. There was Philip, Duke of Wharton, the scorn and wonder of his days, now accepting' a dukedom from King George, and now swearing allegiance to the Pretender, dropping untold thousands at Newmarket, and destined to a miserable end in a Spanish monastery. There was Charles, Duke of Shrewsbury, to whom on her death-bed Queen Anne had delivered the white staff of the Lord Treasurer, and thus frustrated the Jacobite designs of Bolingbroke. There was the Duchess of Roxburgh, who also had her little schemes of treason, and in idler hours told improbable ghost stories, culled from the lucubrations of drunken squires. Superstitious her enemies called her, and malicious withal. There was the charming Lady Essex Robartes, dreading through the long months of autumn the twelve days' travel that should carry her to Christmas festivities in her Cornish home. Among them moved the stately presence of Charles Duke of Bolton, who should have been a stedfast Whig, but some doubted. His father, that madcap Duke who would hold his tongue for a month at a time, and hunted by torchlight, was fifth in descent from Lord Rich. Sixty years later, the opposing political parties were headed by descendants of the Chancellor. Charles James Fox was thundering against his seventh cousin, Lord North. It is hardly probable that their subsequent coalition was due to a recognition of their kinship. With Fox were associated

two others of Lord Rich's line, the Dukes of Richmond. and Devonshire. Living at the same time were John Duke of Roxburgh, the collector of books, and Francis Duke of Bridgewater, the constructor of canals. Of living statesmen may be mentioned the names of the Dukes i if Richmond and Rutland, Lords Ripon, Cowper, Granville, and Hartington, and Sir William Harcourt. So many and so various have been the descendants of Lord Rich.

A word may be added of the lands and houses of Lord Rich. On the death of the fourth Earl of Warwick in 1673 the whole of his property was left to his widow for life. A noble compliment was paid to. Lady Warwick by a great person, who said that her husband had given all his estates to pious uses. On. her death five years later the property of the Riches was divided into many portions. The only part that went to the title was Warwick House in Holborn and the living of St. Bartholomew the Great. The patronage of the Felsted foundation went to the daughters of the third Earl and ultimately devolved upon the youngest of them, the Countess of Nottingham. She left it to her husband, who in turn bequeathed it to the children of his second

marriage. Hence for two centuries past the connexion between Felsted and the house
of Rich has been broken. By far the largest part of the property reverted to Lord
Warwick's sisters. The portions of Lady Scarsdale and Lady Robartes were soon sold.
The house and lands of Leez became the property of the Earl of Manchester. The
preacher of Lady Warwick's funeral sermon concluded his oration witha prayer for
Lord Manchester. " And for your noble Lordship, who are now investing yourself with
her large and noble mantle- – may Elijah's spirit rest upon you as well as his mantle,
that you may rise up anElisha in her place and stead, that Leez may be Leez still, the
seat of Nobleness and Honour, the Hospital of Bounty and Charity, the Sanctuary of
Religion, and" the fear of God, that so you may live, and may live longer, and as much
desired, and when you die (as die you must, for Leez, though a Paradise, hath no Tree
of Life) you may die later and as much lamented as yournoble predecessors." For a
time the splendours of Leez were partially maintained, but the Montagues were not
wealthy, and before many years they had tochoose between Kirabolton and Leez. It
was nowonder that they preferredtheir ancestral home. Leez was sold to the guardians
of Edward Sheffield, Duke of Buckinghamshire, from whom they passed to his half-
brother, Charles Herbert. Herbert sold the property, and it passed into the possession
of Guy's Hospital. The house was demolished save one noble gateway and so much
as would serve for a farm house. The ruin of the gateway is pitiable. The floors will
bear nothing heavier than a pigeon and the walls are wasting away. Four splendid
chimneys, a model toall architects, still bid defiance to time and neglect. Standing
in the courtyard the lover of its history may recall some of its associations. He may
fancy the first Lord Rich, weary of the pomp and circumstance of state, marking the
rise of his lordly mansion and enjoining or approving the mould of newel or mullion.

He may fancy the adherents of Lord Essex planning in hall or corridor the advance
of their patron. He may fancy the boys Robert and Henry Rich at their play, the
one stern even in the pastimes of youth, the other abandoned to gaiety. Here is the
room-where gathered solemn Presbyterian ministers and soldiers. ready to persecnte
or be persecuted as fortune smiled or frowned. Buried under the grass are fragments
of the pavement on which the rough and proud Lucas, overcome with anger and wine,
stumbled and fell ere he rode to his death at Colchester. Hera is the wilderness where
the gentle Countess prayed for patience under the outbursts of her gouty lord. Here
we may sympathise with the grief of the old Earl who saw the hope of his race go
down to an early grave, and again with the grief of the wife and mother who mourned
her husband and her only son. We may turn towards Pelsted and remember how often
the long funeral procession has started along the winding road. Then we shall feel
that here at least the words of Antony haveno fulfilment, and where the Riches rest in
the vaults of Felsted the good is not interred with their bones.

ChapterV. – LISTS.

I. – FELSTED BOYS BEFORE 1800.

JIHE following List is grievously imperfect. As far as can be judged more than
three thousand boys must have passed through Felsted before the year 1800. No
record of them was kept, and we are left to gather their names from College Registers,
from accounts of speech days, and from other chance sources. Every effort has been
made to identify these names and to exclude interlopers: –

Abbreviations. – elk., clerk in orders. b., born. d., died. s., son. r., rector. v., vicar. F., Felsted.

Abdy, Anthony Thomas. s. of Sir William bart. succeeded his father. M. P. for Knaresborough. K. C. d. 1775.

Abdy, John Rutherford. of Albyns. High Sheriff of Essex 1809. d. 1840.

Abdy, Stotherd. M. A. Clk. d. 1773.

Alders, James, b. at Little Easton. sizar of St. John's Camb. 1705. B. A. 1708. M. A. 1712. v. of Great and Little Easton, 1720-1726. v. of Great Sampford 1726-1735. d. 1735.

Alleyn, Charles. b. at Huntingdon, pensioner of St. John's Camb 1685. Alleyn, Gyles, b. in Essex. pensioner of St. John's Camb 1674.

Andrewes, George. b. 1706 at F. of Great Dunmow. d. 1791. Aylmer, Robert, b. at Mugdon Hall. C. C. C. Camb. B. A. 1721. M. A. 1725. v. of Camberwell. Aylmer, Thomas, b. at Mugdon Hall. C. C. C. Camb. B. A. 1717. M. A. 1721. B. D. 1729. Badeley, John? living at Chelmsford in 1801.

Barnard, at F. 1710.

Barrington, Charles, s. of Thomas and Lady Anne (see Rich pedigree). succeeded his brother in baronetcy 1691. M. P. in seven Parliaments for Essex. D. L. and Vice-Admiral of Essex, d. 1715.

Bathurst, Charles. bookseller in London in 1738.

Beadle, Joseph. b. at Barnston. at F. 1656-1661. sizar of Caius 1661.

Beard, at F. 1710.

Bernard, Thomas, b. at Little Bardneld. sizar of St. John's Camb. 1702. B. A. 1705. M. A. 1709. Birch, John. alive in 1800. Birch, Richard. b. 1762 at Roxwell. commoner of New Coll. Ox. 1781. B. A. 1784. M. A. 1788. Birch, William. alive in 1800. Blencowe, John Prescott. b. 1778. d. 1840. Blowre, John. b. at Fairsted. sizar of St. John's Camb 1675. B. A. 1679. M. A. 1683.

Boodle, John, of London, brother of the next.

Boodle, Richard, b. at Ongar. pensioner of Jesus Camb. B. A. Jun. Op. 1800. M. A. 1803. v. of Barkway, Herts, r. of Radstock, Somerset, d. 1853.

Bound, Robert, b. at Chelmsford. pensioner of St. John's Camb 1690. B. A. 1693.

Bragg, at F. 1710.

Bramston, John. b. 1773. went from F. to Eton. Ch. Cli. 1791. B. A. 1795. M. A. 1797. Clk. of Forest Hall. afterwards Bramston-Stane. d. 1857. Bramston, Thomas. b. 1695. at F. 1707. M. P. for Maldou and Essex. Bramston, Thomas Berney. b. 1733. New Coll. Ox. 1751.

M. A. 1754. D. C. L. 1756. M. P. for Essex 1779-1801.

died 1813. Bramston, Thomas Gardiner. b. 1770. New Coll. Ox. 1788.

B. A. 1792. M. P. for Essex 1830-1831. d. 1831. Bramston, William. Queens'
Camb. fellow. D. D. prebendary

of Worcester and r. of Woodham Walter, d. 1735. Brand, Joseph. at F. 1707.
Bridge, Thomas, of Great Dnumow. a large contributor to

the school library. Brock, John? elk. in 1799. Brograve, Thomas, b. 1727 in
Norfolk, bought Springfiel 1

Place. J. P. and D. L. for Essex, d. at Springfield 1810. Budworth, R. at F. 1794.
of Greenstead? Bullock, Edward. b. 1695 at Falkbourne Hall. King's Camb.

LL. B. 1717.

Bullock, John. b. 1703 at Falkbourne Hall.

Bullock, John, of Falkbourne Hall. Colonel. M. P. for

Essex 1802.

Bullock, Josiah. b. 1697 at Falkbourne Hall, which he

inherited from his brother Edward, d. 1752. Bullock, Richard. b. 1701 at
Falkbourne Hall. King's Camb.

B. A. 1724. M. A. 1728. D. D. r. of Streatham, Surrey.

v. of Christ Church, London. Carr, G. D. alive in 1799 and 1804. Carter, Martin,
of Christ's Camb. and Lincoln's Inn. of

Baling Hall. alive in 1707. Carter, Martin, of Bradwell and Witham. coroner for
Essex.

d. 1754.

Carter, Martin. alive in 1796.

Carter, Peter Milbanke. elk. in 1793.

Cater, Beckford. alive in 1798.

Cater, John Rendal. alive in 1764.

Catesbie, at F. 1710.

Cautley, at F. 1797,

Clarence,? alive in 1799.

Clerke, Thomas, b. 1747 at Wethersfield. Magd. Hall. 1763.

B. A. 1767. Cock, Thomas Theophilus. b. 1754. of Messing. High Sheriff
of Essex 1788. d. in Devon 1811.

Cock,

Codd, Edward. of Maldon.

Codd, William, of Maldou.

Collard, Ady. b. 1673. of Albanes in Barnston. d. 1747.

Collard, Joseph. alive in 1663.

Colson, Edward. D. D.

Comyns, John. see p. 47.

Conyers, H. T. alive in 1814.

Conyers, John. alive in 1799. of Copthall?

Cooke, Thomas. see p. 49.

Corsellis, Csesar. b. 1697. of Layer Marney. d. 1761.

Corsellis, Caesar. alive in 1799.

Corsellis, Nicholas, b. 1744 at Wyvenhoe. Lincoln Coll. 1762.

M. A. 1766. Clk. Cowper, John. at F. 1753. Cowper, William. at F. 1764. Cox, Thomas? see p. 46. Creffield, Joseph, b. at Colchester, pensioner of St. Johns Camb 1678. B. A. 1681. M. A. 1685. D. D. 1693.

An ancestor of the Round family.

Cromwell, Henry, b. 1627. d. 1674. see p. 40.

Cromwell, Oliver. b. 1623. d. 164

Cromwell, Richard. b. 1626. d. 1712.

Cromwell, Robert. b. 1621. d. 1639.

Outtertrack, Thomas, b. in London, pensioner of St. John's Camb 1686.

Daniel, William Barker, see p. 45."

Danniells, at F. 1710.

Deeds, elk. in 1803. Perhaps Deedes of Kent, akin to the Brain stons. Be Veil, John. probably s. of the usher. r. of Aldenham, Herts, d. 1808.

Dobie, at F. 1710.

Dod, Edward. b. at Whittlesford, Cambs. at F. 1646-1648.

pensioner of Caius 1650. Dowse, Robert. b. in Loudon. pensioner of St. John's Camb.

1678. B. A. 1681. Drake, Francis. probably son of the chaplain. D. D. alive 1784 and 1818. Ducane, Henry. b. 1786 at Coggeshall. Oriel 1804. B. A.

1808. M. A. 1811. elk. d. 1855. Dyer, Swinerton. b. in London. s. of Sir John S., 2nd bart.

succeeded his father 1701. d. 1736.

Dyson, at F. 1800.

Eve, Richard. at F. 1710. owned land in White Eoding and' elsewhere. Everard, Ralph. b. at Marlesford, Suffolk, at F. 1627-1631.

pensioner of St. John's Camb. 1631. Fairfax, William, b. 1630 at Naworth Castle, Cumberland. son

of William, 2nd Viscount Fairfax of Elmly in peerage of Ireland. succeeded his father 1641. d. 1648. Farr, Samuel. b. at Ashen. at F. 1661-1667. sizar of Caiua

1667. B. A. 1670. M. A. 1674. Fellowes, Robert. see p. 59.

Fellowes, William. b. 1767 at Danbury. Ch. Ch. 1785. Lincoln's Inn, 1788. Firmin, Nathaniel. b. at Slialford. sizar of Cains 1664. B. A

1667. Fitch, William. b. at Wethersfield. at F. 1669-1675. sizar of Caius 1675. B. A. 1679.

Fitch, William. of Danbury Place 1799.

Forster, Edward? alive in 1799.

Foster, John. at F. 1708.

Frere, Bartholomew. see p. 60.

Frere, George. alive in 1818. Perhaps too late for this list.

Frere, William, b. 1775. at F. May 1784- Dec. 1790. after-

wards at Eton. Trinity Coll. Camb. 1794. Craven
Scholar and Browne's Medallist 1796. Browne's Medal-
list 1797. 1st Chancellor's Medallist and B. A. 1798.
Sen. Op. 1799. M. A. and fellow of Downing 1801.
LL. D. called to the bar Middle Temple 1802. serjeant-
at-law 1809. Master of Downing 1812-1836. Vice-
Chancellor of Cambridge 1819. Recorder of Bury St.
Edmund's, d. 1836.
Fytch, Thomas. of Woodham Walter 1754. High Sheriff of
Essex.
<Jascoyne, Bamber. b. 1727. s. of Sir Crisp, kt. Queen's
Ox. 1743. called to the bar Lincoln's Inn 1750. M. P.
for Maldon 1761-63, for Midhurst 1765-70, for Weobley
1770-74, for Trnro 1774-84, for Bossiney 1784-8(5.
commissioner of trade 1763. a lord of the admiralty
1779. receiver- general of customs and verdurer of
Waltham Forest, d. 1791. an ancestor of the Marquis
of Salisbury.
Oepp, George Asser. b. 1768. of Chelmsford. <1. 1856.
Gepp, Thomas Frost, b. 1767. of Chelmsford. d. 1832.
Gibson, Samuel. b. at Little Waldingfield, Suffolk, at F.
1641-1644. sizar of St. John's Camb. 1644.
Gibson, at F. 1710.
Glascock, Christopher. see p. 17.
Glascock, Christopher, b. at Ipswich, s. of the chaplain.
scholar of Caius 1667. B. A. 1670. M. A. 1674.
Glascock, Francis. b. at Little Canfield. sizar of St. John's
Camb. 1665.
Glascock, John. Queen's Camb. B. A. 1663. M. A. 1667.
usher at F. 1664-1678.
Olascock, Thomas. b. 1665 at F. s. of the chaplain. of
Bedel's Hall in Writtle. town clerk of Colchester, d.
1727.
Glascock, William. at F. 1710.
Glascock. (probably other sons of the chaplain were under
him at F. their names were Isaac, b. 1657, Charles, b.
1661, George, b. 1663).
Godbold, John. b. at Sudbury, Suffolk. s. of the next. Magd.
Ox. 1754.
Godbold, Richard, left F. 1710. r. of All Saints', Sndbnry.
v. of Margaret Rodiug 1733-1747. d. 1747.
Goodall, Joseph. at F. after 1739.
Green, Thomas. at F. 1709-1710.
Gretton, H. Pemb. Camb. B. A. 1775. elk. in 1799.
Gretton, Mark. Pemb. Camb. B. A. 1738. M. A. 1742. usher

at F. 1741-1752. cnrate of F. 1746-1748. v. of Good.
Easter 1746-1762. v. of Margaret Roding 1747-1762.
incumbent of Little Dunmow 1749-1762. d. 1762. his
portrait is in the well-known print of the Flitch of
Bacon.
Gretton, Phillips. b. 1677. Trin. Coll. Camb. B. A. 1697.
M. A. 1701. D. D. 1732. r. of Springfield 1703-1744.
author of some pamphlets on controversial theology.
d. 1744.
Griffenhoofe, G. elk. in 1799.
Griffenhoofe, Nicholas. St. John's Camb. B. A. 1741. M. A.
1749. r. of Kelvedou Hatch 1758-1760. v. of Stow
Mareys 1761.
Griffith, Guyon. Clare. B. A. 1750. M. A. 1754. D. D. 1766.
Gurdon, John, at F. 1709.
Guyon, at F. 1710.
Hanbury, Osgood. of Oldfield Grange in 1801.
Hanoe, Henry. at F. 1763 and 1764. of Maldon in 1801.
Hance, John, of Maldon in 1799
Harington, James. b. at Great Maplestead. at F. 1640-1643.
sizar of St. John's Camb. 1643.
Harrison, at F. 1710.
Harrison, at F. 1710.
Harrison, John Haynes. St. John's Camb. B. A. 1777. M. A.
1780. of Copford Hall?
Haselfoot, Robert Clere. at F. 1797. of Boreham.
Hawker, at F. 1710.
Heath, Bailey. of Stanstead Hall. High Sheriff of Essex 1747.
Herringham, at F. 1802.
Heywood, Edmund. b. at Wimbish. sizar of St. John's
Camb. 1682.
Holingsworth, at F. 1710. of Thundridgebury, Herts?
Holies, William. b. 1664. s. of Gilbert, 3rd Earl of Clare.
killed at Luxemburgh 1684.
Holmested, Thomas. at F. 1710. of Braintree.
Holmested, T. alive in 1814.
Horsemanden, Harrington. at F. 1710.
Horsemanden, Samuel. b. 1699 at Bromley. Ch. Ch. 1716.
B. A. 1719. B. C. L. 1726. v. of Haseley, Warwick, 1724-
1732. r. of Purleigh 1726. r. of Woodham Walter
1732. J. P. for Essex. d. 1769. a printed sermon of his
dated 1744 is in the British Museum.
Horsemanden, at F. 1710.
Houblon, John Archer, of Hallingbury. High Sheriff of Essex
1801.

How, Richard. of Stondon Massey in 1711.

Hughes, Owen. b. at Cambridge. at F. 1641-1644. Scholar
of Caius 1644.

Hughes, William Lewis. afterwards Lord Dinorben. see p. 55.

Hunt, William. alive in 1801.

Jackson, Francis James. see p. 57.

Jackson, John. alive in 1801.

James, John, alive in 1801.

Jenner, at F. 1710.

Johnson, James. b. in Whitechapel. at F. 1653-1657. St.
John's Camb. 1657.

Joscelyn, Edward. s. of Sir Robert bart. r. of High Boding.
d. 1732.

Joynonr, at F. 1710.

Joynour, at F. 1710.

Joynonr, at F. 1710.

Kidby, Edmund. r. of East and West Hanningfield 1689.
prebendary of Islington, d. 1718.

Kinsman, at F. 1710. probably Josias K. of Ardern
Hall.

Kortright, C. H. of Fryerning in 1801.

Kortright, W. of St. Leonard, Fryerning, 1820.

Kynaston, H. at F. 1797.

Kyuaston, Roger. St. John's Camb. B. A. 1798. M. A- 1801.

Kynaston, Thomas. of Witham Grove in 1801.

Lawrence, William. alive in 1801.

Leader, Charles. b. at Great Dunmow. New Coll. Ox. 1715.
B. A. 1719. M. A. 1723. r. of Evenlode, Worcester, 1739?

Leapingwell, George. curate of Little Dunmow 1795-1801. v. of
High Easter 1815-1849. d. 1849.

Leapingwell, John, alive in 1799.

Le Blanc, G. at F. 1794.

Leigh, John. b. at Groton, Suffolk. sizar of St. John's Camb.
1645.

Lescollet, at F. 1710.

Lloyd, John. v. of Epping 1710-1753. v. of Stapleford Tany
1732-1753. d. 1753.

Longe, R. R. elk. in 1801.

Luckin, s. of Sir William bart. of Messing. at F. 1710.

Luckin, brother of the above. at F. 1710.

Lukin, William b. 1709 at Great Easton. Peterhouse 1727.
M. B. 1733. d. 1755.

Lukin, William. alive in 1801.

Lumley, James, s. of Sir Martin bart. of Great Bardfield.
pensioner of St. John's Camb. 1649.

Lumley, Thomas, brother of the above. fellow commoner of
St. John's Camb. 1646.
Lydiatt, John. b. 1705. at F. s. of the chapain.
Lydiatt, Thomas. probably nephew of the chaplain. Cath.
Hall. LL. B. 1717.
Lynn, W. 1794.
Mann, at P. 1710.
Mann, at F. 1710.
Manning, F. at F. 1606.
Marriott, at F. 1710.
Marriott, captain in 1796.
Marshall, at F. 1710.
Massingberd, Samuel, b. 1749 at Gunby, Line. Univ. Coll.
Ox. 1767. demy and fellow of Magd. B. A. 1771. M. A.
1774. usher at F. 1775-1776. curate of F. 1775-1780.
drowned in the Delaware 1781.
Maysent, or Meisant. B. of John of Booking. at F.
1710. d. young.
Meyricke, John. b. in Pembrokeshire. New Coll. Ox. 1754.
Mildmay, Henry. b. 1620. s. of Sir Henry bart. of Graces,
Baddow. M. P. for Essex. said to have been named one
of the court to try Charles I. d. 1692.
Mills, William. alive in 1799.
Morgan, John? r. of Chelmsford. d. 1815.
Morritt, John. at F. 1753.
Newman, John. elk. in 1794.
Newman, Richard. alive in 1799.
Newman, Thomas. elk. in 1799.
Newton, John. b. in Yorkshire. pensioner of St. John's
Camb. 1632.
Newton, at F. 1710.
Nottidge, G. alive in 1799.
Nottidge, John. v. of Ashingdon in 1795.
Nottidge, Josias. of Booking. High Sheriff of Essex in 1790.
Nottidge, Josias, s. of the above.
Page, John, at F. 1764.
Parker, Charles. alive in 1799.
Parker, Comyns, at F. 1794. d. 1843.
Parker, John Oxley. of Chelmsford.
Peachie, Thomas, at F. after 1694.
Pepper, Michael. of Bigwood in 1801.
Pepys, John, at F. 1710. of Spain's Hall in Yeldham till 1749.
Peyton, John, at F. 1760.
Phillips, C. b. 1729 at Walthamstow. B. N. C. 1745. B. A. from
St. Alban's Hall 1749. v. of Terling. d. 1801.

Phillips, Spencer. of Reff ham's Lodge in 1811?
Pigot, John Coe. alive in 1799.
Pledger, Elias. received an exhibition from F. to Camb. 1639-
1643. a preacher in Essex. r. of St. Antholin's, London,
1659, ejected 1662. had a conventicle at the Pheasant
in Friday Street, and afterwards a meeting house in
Lothbury. d. 1676. Some sermons of his are in the
British Museum.
Potter, James, b. at Colne. pensioner of St. John's, Camb-
1705.
Powlter, at F. 1710.
Pngh, at F. 1710. perhaps Robert v. of Runwell.
Pyke, Richard. Trin. Hall. B. A. 1719. brother of the next.
Pyke, William. Cath. Hall. B. A. 1715. of Baythorn Park.
Beynardson, at F. 1710.
Richardson, Anthony. at F. 1753. perhaps s. of Richard v.
of Finchingfield.
Ripley, at F. 1799.
Bound, James, b. 1764. of Birch Hall. elk. d. 1809.
Rons, George. Trin. Coll. Camb. B. A. 1807. M. A. 1811. elk.
Rons, at F. 1799. probably brother of the above.
Sannderson, William. d. 1579 at F. the first recorded
Felstedian.
Saunders, Matthew. b. at Barnston. sizar of St. John's,
Camb. 1632.
Savil, John. at F. 1708. barrister at law. of Stisted HalU
d. 1735.
Scarlet, Edward. b. at Canfield. at F. 1637-1640. Scholar of
Caius, 1640.
Searle, Andrew, at F. 1710. of Chambers in Epping. drowned
1762.
Searle, George. brother of the above. Magd. Camb. B. A.
1716. M. A. 1720.
Sherwill, Thomas. fellow of Christ's. B. A. 1693. M. A. 1697.
D. D. 1717. Some sermons of his are in the British
Museum, one on the right use of education, preached at
F. 1710, and a Latin pastoral in Lacrymae Cantabrigienses
1694.
Skynner, Stephen. at F. 1710. of Walthamstow in 1753.
Smijth, William. s. of Sir William 6th bart. succeeded his
father 1777. Colonel of W. Essex militia, d. 1823.
Smith, Benjamin. b. at Great Dunmow. at F. 1652-1659.
sizar of St. John's Camb. 1659. B. A. 1663. M. A. 1667.
Smith, Charles. alive in 1799.
Smith, at F. 1710. perhaps s. of Thomas of Great

Bardfield.

Sparhawk, Samuel. b. 1657 at Black Notley. at F. 1667-1669. sizar of Gains 1669. B. A. 1672. M. A. 1676.

Sparrow, John. b. 1662. Christ's Camb. 1679. called to the bar 1686. of Gosfield Place. d. 1720.

Staines, at F. 1710.

Staines, at F. 1710.

Stanee, E. C. alive in 1799.

Sterry, S. H. alive in 1799.

Sterry, Wasing. alive in 1799.

Stileman, Robert. at F. 1707 and 1708. probably of Snettis-ham, Norfolk.

Strutt, John. b. 1702. of Terling. M. P. for Maldon. d. 1790.

Strutt, John. d. 178.

Strutt, Joseph Holden. husband of 1st Lady Rayleigh. colonel. d. 1845.

Strutt, William Goodday. deputy governor of Stirling Castle-1796. major-general 1798. governor of Quebec, d. 1848.

Tabrum, Arthur, alive in 1801.

Thorpe, George. b. in London, sizar of Caius 1653. after-wards fellow.

Thurlow, J. elk. in 1801.

Tillingham, Edward. b. at Great Dunmow. at F. 1628-1631. St. John's Catnb. 1631.

Tindall, Robert, at P. 1797.

Toke, J. b. 1771 at Barnston. Bmman. B. A. 1790.

Toke, William. v. of Feleted 1797. r. of Barnston 1807.

Townson, Thomas, see p. 51.

Trivett, William. s. of the chaplain, afterwards at West-minster, elk.

Tufnell, William? of Langleys in 1801.

Tyler, John. at F. 1753. alive in 1801.

Tyrrell, Charles. alive in 1708.

Tyrrell, Charles. b. 1723. s. of Sir John bart. succeeded his father 1729. d. at F. 1735.

Tyrrell, John. s. of Sir Charles, bart. of Springfield. succeeded his father, d. 1729.

Tyrrell, John. s. of the above. succeeded his brother 1735. high sheriff of Essex 1749. d. 1766.

Tyrrell, John. b. 1762. of Boreham. created a bart. 180!). high sheriff of Essex 1827. d. 1832.

Tyrrell, John Tyssen. b. 1795. s. of the above. succeeded his father 1832. M. P. for N. Essex.

Tyrrell, at F. 1710. probably son of Charles.

Underwood, Thomas, b. at Thornage, Norfolk. sizar of Cains

1637.

Vachell, Tanfield. Pemb. Camb. B. A. 1787. M. A. 1790.

Vachell, William? b. 1735. of Hingeston, Camb. and Coptf old
Hall. high sheriff of Camb. and Hunt. 1783. d. 1807.

Vandergoe, John, alive in 1799.

Wakeham, Charles. Christ's Camb. B. A. 1782. M. A. 1785.

Waldron, Francis Storrard. b. at Stapleford Abbot. pensioner
of St. John's Camb. 1682.

Walford, John. alive in 1801.

Walford, Luke W. of Little Bardfield. high sheriff of Essex
1815.

Wallace, Thomas, elk. in 1802.

Wallis, John, see p. 37.

Wangford, at F. 1710. probably of Berwicks in Topes-
field.

Wang-ford, at F. 1710. brother of the above.

Western, Charles Callis. afterwards Lord Western, see p. 56.

. Western, Elias. alive in 1794.

Western, Shirley. b. 1769. brother of Lord W. Queen's
Camb. B. A. 1791. M. A. 1794. r. of Rivenhall. d.
1824.

Western, Thomas Walsingham. b. 1748. Queen's Camb.
LL. B. 1773. r. of Rivonhall.

Wheeler, at F. 1710.

Wilkes, John. of Loft's Hall. high sheriff of Essex 1819.

Wilson, at F. 1710. probably of Jenkins in Stisted.

Wilson, at F. 1710.

Wiltshire, – at F. 1710.

Wolfe, John. of Turges in Writtle in 1799.

"Wood, Stephen. alive in 1799.

Woodroffe, John. r. of Cranham 1753.

Woodroffe, Thomas. at F. 1710. s. of Thomas, v. of Felsted:

Wragg, Christopher. b. at Barnston. scholar of Cains 1670.
B. A. 1672.

Wragg, Thomas. b. in London. brother of the above. at F.
1667-1673. scholar of Caius 1673. B. A. 1673. M. A.
1677.

Wright, Henry, b. 1660. s. of Sir Henry 1st bart. succeeded.
his father 1663. of Dagenham. d. 1681.

Wright, John? b. 1763. of Kelvedon Hall. d. 1826.

Wright, Peter. b. 1767. of Hatfield Priory.

Wynn, John, of Maesyneaulde, Merioneth, in 1785.

Young, James? alive in 1799.

II. – CHAPLAINS OB HEAD MASTERS
WITH THE DATES OF THEIR APPOINTMENT.

Allthechaplainshavebeenclerksinorders.

Henry Sayer or Sawer.

Wharton?

Thomas Bogerson. v. of Felsted.

Daubney or Dabney. Perhaps Henry. Ch: Ch: SI. A. 1553.

John Berryman. 1566. St. John's Camb. B. A. 1557. M. A. 1562.

Henry Greenwood. 1576. Fellow of St. John's Camb. B. A. 1567. M. A. 1571.

George Manning. 1597. C. C. C. Camb. B. A. 1580.

Martin Holbeach. 1627. Queen's Camb. B. A. 1621. M. A. 1624.

Skingle. 1649. Perhaps incumbent of Little Dunmow.

Christopher Glascock. 1650. Cath. Hall Camb. B. A. 1634. M. A. 1638.

Simon Lydiatt. 1690. Ch: Ch: B. A. 1680. M. A. 1683.

Hugh Hutchin. 1712. Ch:Ch: B. A. 1698. M. A. 1701.

JohnWyatt. 1725. Ch:Ch: B. A. 1717. M. A. 1720.

William Drake. 1750. Ch: Ch: B. A. 1744. D. D.?

William Trivett. 1778. Ch: Ch: B. A. 1767. M. A. 1770.

William John Carless. 1794. Merton. B. A. 1793.

Edmund Squire. 1813. Christ's Camb. B. A. 1801. M. A. 1804.

Thomas Surridge. 1835. T. C. D. B. A. 1810. LL. D. 1834.

Albert Henry Wratislaw. 1850. Fellow of Christ's Camb. B. A. 1844. M. A. 1847.

William Stanford Grignon. 1855. Trin. Coll. Camb. B. A. 1846. M. A. 1849.

Delaval Shafto Ingram. 1876. St. John's Camb. B. A. 1862. M. A. 1865.

III. – USHERS.

John Bycknor. 1569.

Gyles Raymond. 1579.

Foyner or Joyner. 1591.

Arthur Raymond. 1595. retired on a pension: d. 1637 at Dunmow.

Linsel. 1626.

Seton. 1628. elk.

Hills. 1629.

[Probably some names are missing after this year.]

Ardley. 1650.

Ingart. 1658.

Foyner or Joyner. 1658.

John Goodwin. 1662. St. John's Camb. M. A. 1663.

John Glascock. 1664. see p.
Cressel. 1678.
David Price. 1693. Trin. Coll. Camb. B. A. 1691. d. 1731.
Hans, de Veil. 1731. Probably son of Sir Thomas. Emman.
Camb. B. A. 1724. v. of Baling 1732-1741. v. of F.
1740-1741. d. 1741.
Mark Gretton. 1741. see p. 118.
William Drake. 1752. King's Camb. B. A. 1752. elk.
Chaloner Bing Baldock. 1773. Christ's Camb. B. A. 1773.
M. A. 1790.
John Barlow Seale. 1774. Fellow of Christ's Camb. B. A.
1774. M. A. 1777.
Samuel Massingberd. 1774. See p. 121.
[Some names missing.]
"William Gordon. 1778. Christ's Camb. B. A. 1777. M. A. 1780.
curate of F. 1777-1780.
. John Clark. 1786. Trin. Coll. Camb. B. A. 1784. M. A. 1788.
curate of F. 1784.
William Worthington. 1788. Trin. Coll. Camb. B. A. 1787.
curate of F. 1788-1790.
– s – Gumming. 1794. elk. Houlditch. 1797. elk?
Thomas Brereton. 1799. Merton. B. A. 1798. elk.
John Simpson. 1804. curate of F. 1806-1816.
James Charnock. 1813.
J. F. Roberts. 1815. St. John's Camb. B. A. 1815. M. A. 1820.
elk.
William Wilkinson. 1820. Cath. Hall Camb. B. A. 1820.
elk. d. 1824.
Joseph Edwards. 1824. Trin. Coll. Camb. B. A. 1824. M. A.
1835. afterwards second master of King's College
School. elk.
James Crocker. 1825. Trin. Coll. Cam. B. A. 1825. M. A.
1828. d. 1876.
Richard Heighway Kirby. 1842. St. John's Camb. B. A. 1840.
M. A. 1843. see p. 33.
GLOSSARIUM FELSTEUICUM.
As no local history can ignore dialectical idiosyncrasies, the learned will perhaps
pardon a list of words that are believed to be all our own.
Buck: jolly, happy. From buxom.
DrawBound: to cuff, box the ears.
Drive: an exclamation implying that news is stale. " Oh, do
drive!"FainLO: a phrase used to assert a claim to a seat that is
vacated for a moment.
FuoPlant: the common henbane, hyoscyamus niger.
Hots: pennies or halfpennies.

Nip: a bucolic, an outsider. cp. East Anglian " nipper."

NoLoss: the same as fain lo.

Pog: face.

Stub: to kick, to kick a football about.

Tetra: the best point, the " record." " He ran beyond the tetra."

Tip: a false report, a mistake in translating.

Tollt: a candle or dip. From tallow.

Vic: " cave," a note of warning.

Wanker: a herring, a bloater.

PUBLICATIONS.

The Ancient Sepulchral Monuments of Essex. ByFred. Cha. ncrllor, Esq., P. R. I. B. A. Imp. 4to, cloth, $3 3s. to Subscribers.*In the Press.*

Durrant's Handbook for Essex. A Guide to all the Principal Objects of Interest in each Parish in the County, for the use of Tourists and others; with an Introduction treating of its History, Geology, Area, Population, Dialect. Antiquities, Worthies, Natural History. &c. By MrilBBCkkisty. Author of the "Trado-Siirns of E<sex." &c. With jta;>s, 2s. (id. nctt, post free. " Accu.-ate and Trustworthy." I>. u/y*Telejraph.*

The Trade-Signs of Essex. A Popular Account of the Origin and Meanings of the Public House anil other Signs, nov or formerly found in the County of Essex. With illustrations. ByMillekChuistv. Demy 8vo, cloth, 7s. 6d. uett

Rays of Light for Sick and Weary ones. Compiled*by*EdithL. Wans. With a Preface by Rev. PkkbendibyHuiroy. Cron-n 8vo, cloth, 6s.

Homespun Yarns. ByEdwinColler. Crown 8vo, cloth, 3s. 6d.

Royal Illustrated History of Eastern England. Civil, Military, Politic il, and Ecclesiastical, including a Survey ol' the Eastern Counties. and Memoirs of County Families and Eminent Men of every pe;-io 1. By A. D. Bayne, Esq. With many illustrations. Two vols. large Svo, cloth. 21s.

Domesday Book relating to Essex. Translated by the late T. C. Chisbnhale-mahsh, Esq. 4to, cloth, 21s.*Only a feu: Copies unsold.*

John Noakes and Mary Styles; or, An Essex Calf s Visit to Tiptres Races A Poom in the Essex Dialect. By the lateCharlesClauk, of Totham Hall. With a Glossary and Portrait. "(Id.

The History of Rochford Hundred, Essex. Now Publishing in Parts, 6d. each. Tol. 1, I5s. 6d.; vol. 2, 18s. nott. ByPhilipBkntok, Esq.

Short Notes on the Book of Exodus. By the Kev. W. J. Packs, M. A., Vicar of Feering. Seved, 7d.; cloth, Is.

Durrant'sThreepennyAtlas.

Durrant'

sPennyChelmsfordDrawingBook.

Durrant's Exercise Book. Id., 2d., and 4d.

Sermons by the late Ven. Archdeacon Mildmay. With a Preface by theBishopOfSr. Albans.3s. 6d.

A First Catechism of Botany. ByJohnGiB3s. Second Edition. Price 6cl.

The Symmetry of Flowers. ByJohnGibbs. Price 4d.

Durrant's Handy Farm Labour Book. New Edition, with Daily Diary (commencing either Monday or Saturday). 3s. 6d.

Confirmation or, The Laying on of Hands upon those that are Baptized. Now Edition Id., sewed.

Forms and Services used in the Diocese of St. Albans. Published by Authority. Lists on application.

EDMUND DUEEANT & Co., 90 High-St., Chelmsford.

The People's History of Essex. The only Reliable Modern History of the kind. In one volura3, 8vo, 61t pages, Half-bound in Calf, Gilt Lettered, with a Map, price 13s. 6d.; or in Cloth Covers, 11s. Comprises a narrative of public and political events in the County from the earliest ages to the date of publication, wiih Descriptive Sketches of Antiquities. Ruins, and the Seats of the N ibility and Country Gantry – many written specially for this Work. Also, a History of the Hundreds and Boroughs, with a list of I'arishes, probable origin of their names, number of Acres, Population, As-essment to County Rate, and Tithe Rent-charge, Rectorial and Vicarial; aad an epitome of the Parochial Charities.

Morant's History of Essex. Slorant's History of Essex contains a record of all the principal Estats. s and Manorial Rights, with their descents from a very early period, whether to Heirs at Law, by Will, or by Alienation. It also furnishes the best History of the Religious Foundations, Free Schools, Charity Schools, Almshouses, their Endowments and Charitable Gifts; Ecclesiastical Honeflcns and Chapelries, Tithes, &c. A few copies of the facsimile reprint of this valuable County Work being left in the hands of the publishers, they offer thorn- at the following very reduced prices: –

Large paper copy. Small paper copy.

As published in 120 Nos.* $00 $1 10 0

In cloth, two vols 2 12 6 220

Half-bound and Lettered, two vols. 300 2 10 0

Calf and Lettered, two void 400 350

*The large paper copy, which is accompanied by a mip, was published at$10; the smalt paper copy at$7 10s.Original copies sell for$l(ito$20.

The Essex Almanac and County Directory. Published annually in December, tu theOdice of the " Essex County Chronicle," 98, High-street, Chelm. si'ord, and to be obtained of all Booksellers. In crown 8vo, price 6d.; Limp Cloth, Is.; Cloth Boards, Is. 6d. By post 3d. extra. ThisAnnual County Directorygives particulars of every town and principal village in the County – each introduced by a brief description, accompanied with all requisite information as to the public life of the several places. After the usual Calendar matter are Lists of the Nobility and Gentry, with their family pedigrees; of Magistrates and Clergymen; of Countv Volunteer Forces, and of the Officers of the Diocese; of Nonconformist Ministers and of Roman Catholic Churches; of public Benevolent and Religious Institutions; of Schools and School Boards; Polling Districts; and so nuch other useful information, that hardly a fact of importance connecteJ with the County has been omitted. Th Book is rea'ly what it claims to be, and the information afforded is both accurate and exhaustive. No public office, gentleman's library, or counting-house can be considered completely furnished unless a copy of the*Emiex Almanac*is close at hand.

Special "Essex Almanac" Maps of Essex. A Large Map of Essex, specially coloured to illustrate some phase of county history, and alone worth m >re than is charged for the whole work, is given nnually with each copy of the Aim mac. Appended is a list of Maos thus published, with the year of their publication attached. The series forms a valuable illustration of the later history of the county.

1830 Parliamentary Divisions
1881 Hunting Countries
1882 Hailways and Telegraphs
18S3 Poor Law Unions
1885 Petty Sessional Divisions
188J rolling Districts, &c.
1836 New Electoral Divisions
1337) Electoral Divisions and Polling
1888 j Places
1-389 County Council Divisions
1890 Ditto, and New Railway Lines
"Essex County Chronicle" Office, 98 High-Street, Chelmsford.